FOUNDATIONS OF SOCIOLOGY

FOUNDATIONS OF
SOCIOLOGY

by GEORGE A. LUNDBERG

UNIVERSITY OF WASHINGTON

DAVID McKAY COMPANY, INC.   NEW YORK

FOUNDATIONS OF SOCIOLOGY

LIBRARY OF CONGRESS CATALOG CARD NUMBER: 64-10331

MANUFACTURED IN THE UNITED STATES OF AMERICA

PREFACE

THIS REVISED AND ABRIDGED EDITION consists of Part I (Chapters 1 to 4) of my *Foundations of Sociology* (Macmillan, 1939), plus a brief epilogue representing a comparison of two current systems of sociological conceptual schemes. The original edition was given its title because the book was concerned primarily not with the substantive content of sociology but with the assumptions, postulates, and premises that underlie the theoretical and empirical work necessarily involved in the development of a natural science of sociology. This is even more true of this edition. The original title, therefore, is also suitable for this edition.

Neither the original edition nor the present edition purports to be a systematic treatise on sociology or on the philosophy of science. The intention of the original volume as well as of this edition was, and is, to expound the philosophy of natural science only insofar as that philosophy is basic to the development of a natural science of sociology. To do this as briefly as possible, it was found desirable to let the text for the most part take the form of a refutation of specific allegations that have been made as to the inapplicability of the methods and logic of natural science to human social phenomena. This is obviously a much smaller undertaking than would be a full treatment of the philosophy of science.

The position here presented doubtless partakes more of some "schools" of philosophy than of others. The extent to which the positivism of Comte, for example, resembles the viewpoint here adopted I

v

have reviewed elsewhere ("Contemporary Positivism in Sociology," *American Sociological Review,* Vol. IV, No. 1, February, 1939, pp. 42-55), and it is not here repeated. In short, the historical development and relationship of the various "schools" of philosophy are not regarded as particularly relevant to our present undertaking.

In the quarter of a century that has elapsed since the publication of the original edition, many of the more common objections to the argument here undertaken have become rather obsolete. For example, the argument regarding the possibility and desirability of quantification in the social sciences is now perhaps chiefly of historical interest (see p. 83). Other aspects of the philosophy and methodology of science are of as much interest today as they were at the time of the publication of the original volume. In any event, it may safely be said that this edition represents examples of the kinds of theoretical questions that agitate and have agitated sociologists and philosophers of science during the second and present quarters of this century. Some of these questions will, in my opinion, continue to crop up and frustrate inquiry as long as they are not subjected to more fundamental semantic inquiry than they have been to date.

The original text and its footnotes at the end of each chapter are reproduced in this edition almost without any change. New material appears chiefly in Chapter I, Section C, 8 (The Non-Ethical Nature of Science); in Chapter IV, Section C (Obstacles to the Development of Sociological Laws); and in the Epilogue. The footnotes at the bottom of the pages represent comments on material in the first edition as well as on the new material. These new footnotes also refer to significant recent literature that has appeared since publication of the First Edition.

GEORGE A. LUNDBERG

University of Washington
Seattle
January, 1964

TABLE OF CONTENTS

FOUNDATIONS OF SOCIOLOGY

Chapter I

THE POSTULATES OF SCIENCE AND
THEIR IMPLICATIONS FOR SOCIOLOGY

A. Science as a Technic of Adjustment

HUMAN SOCIOLOGY DEALS with the communicable adjustment technics which human groups have developed in their long struggle to come to terms with each other and with the rest of their environment. Science is, in the fields where it has been tried, the most conspicuously successful of these technics. As a human adjustment technic, science is primarily a *sociological* subject. Hence, if we start out with a brief consideration of this technic, we are not going outside our subject, but into a very vital aspect of it. Furthermore, since we wish to attempt to use this technic in the study of human group-behavior itself, it is not only permissible but necessary to consider first the implications of that approach.

All inquiry begins with an experienced tension or imbalance of some sort in the inquiring organism. "Tension" and "imbalance" are words used to describe the result of an imperfect adjustment. "Adjustment" is in turn a word used to describe the situation under which the activities of an organism come to rest or equilibrium.[1] The latter we define, as in physics, as the state of maximum probability in any organism or other system. We shall also refer to this state of maximum probability as the "normal" in any societal situation.

1

When certain tensions are formulated verbally they tend to take the form of a question. The tentative, experimental answer to this question is called a hunch, a guess, a hypothesis, or a postulate. A tentative answer of this kind serves as a basis for the orderly assembling of data which will establish more firmly, modify, or refute the hypothesis. A hypothesis which is corroborated by repeated observations made by all qualified observers is thereupon called a principle or a law. Hunches, hypotheses, and guesses are produced, of course, by the responses of the organism to some situation, i.e., through data of experience, just as are the more adequately supported generalizations called principles or laws. "Hunches" differ from "principles" only in that the former rest upon more subjective (i.e., private, unverified), transitory, and quantitatively inadequate data. These characteristics frequently have misled men to believe that "hunches" are somehow generated spontaneously in the "mind"— a view which is here repudiated in favor of the position stated above.[2]

In its maturest form the content of science consists of a body of verified propositions so related that under given rules (logic) the system is self-consistent and compatible with empirical observation. The more universally applicable these propositions are, i.e., the greater the variety of phenomena covered by the propositions, the more adequate is our knowledge of the field which they cover. Thus, nearly all empirically observed behavior of bodies from the point of view of their movement in space and time are "covered" by the general "principles" of physics. That is, events as "different" (from some points of view) as a man falling from a twentieth-story window, a bullet fired into the air from a rifle, or drops of water in a rain storm, are all "explained" by the same basic principle.

No two cases of any of these events are ever identical in all respects nor are the natural conditions under which they occur ever the same. Yet by a process of ignoring all this variety and concentrating our attention on some single characteristic or aspect of the event (abstracting), we can make general statements that are equally true for all falling men, all rain drops, and all projectiles. This standardization of widely different events is achieved either through actual laboratory controls or through symbolic, usually statistical, devices. Thus are myriads of unique events of the most heterogeneous nature described, classified, summarized, and "explained" by showing that they are only special cases of a general rule or law already "understood" and terms of which we have become accustomed to make adjustments to these events. We say that anything is "explained" or "understood" when we have reduced a situation to elements and correlations with which we are so familiar that we accept them as a matter of course so that our curiosity rests. By "element" we mean any component which we do not consider necessary or possible further to analyze. Understanding a situation means, from the operational point of view, discovering familiar elements and correlations between them.[3]

As a result of his familiarity with the principles which govern (describe, explain) most of the events in the so-called "physical"[4] universe, man adjusts today to these events with relative emotional equanimity. That is, his curiosity and other adjustments come to rest relatively easily and without the fears, doubts, angers, and magical practices which accompanied his adjustment to these events in pre-scientific times. The absence of reliable principles brings forth a vast amount of trial-and-error blundering and emotional squirmings in social adjustments as compared to our relatively systematic adjustments to the "physical" world. Scientific knowledge operates, therefore, as a sort of mental hygiene in the fields where it is applied. If the morning paper reports an earthquake, an eclipse, a storm, or a flood, these events are immediately referred to their proper place in the framework of science, in which their explanation, i.e., their relationship to other events, has already been worked out. Hence each new event of this character calls for very little, if any, "mental" or "emotional" strain upon the organism so far as our intellectual adjustment to it as an event is concerned.

Political and social upheavals, on the other hand, such as wars, revolutions, and crime are to most people a matter of shock and much personal recrimination and other emotionalism. Yet these societal events are "natural" in the same sense that "physical" events are "natural." "Natural" and "physical" are of course merely words by which we describe a relatively objective (corroborated) type of adjustment to the phenomena so designated. Unfortunately, it is at present very generally assumed that these terms represent not merely a type of adjustment technic on our part, but that such terms as "physical" and "natural" are inherent characterizations of *some* phenomena in the universe but not of others. The other type or types of data are variously and vaguely designated as "social," "cultural," "mental," and "spiritual." These terms, instead of being regarded as describing those situations to which we make at present a relatively subjective and emotional type of adjustment, are likewise *attributed to data as inherent characteristics.* The result of this semantic confusion has been a most mischievous separation of fields of knowledge into the "natural" and "physical" on the one hand as against the "social" and "cultural" (mental, non-material, spiritual) on the other. As a consequence, it has been assumed that the methods of studying the former field are not applicable to the latter. The generally admitted lag in the progress of the "social" as contrasted with the "physical" sciences has been a further result.

The history of science consists largely of the account of the gradual expansion of realms of the "natural" and the "physical" at the expense of the "mental" and the "spiritual." One by one "spiritual" phenomena have become "physical." This is not the place to review that history. It is readily available elsewhere and its implications for the point here under discussion are reasonably clear. The evolution of the concept of the "soul" is especially relevant, because its final stage of transition or translation by way of the "mind" into purely "physical" concepts is still under way. The resistance which this transition is encountering in some quarters is especially instructive because it illustrates the widespread linguistic confusion as to the nature of verbal symbols.

B. *The Postulates of Science*

TO PREVENT CONSTANT DIGRESSION and misunderstandings from arising, it is necessary in this connection to call attention explicitly to the postulates and their corollaries upon which we proceed. This will seem to some to be a needless repetition and elaboration of the obvious. To others the postulates will seem unjustified. The implications of these assumptions will be set forth in this and subsequent chapters. Only as much of the reasoning will be given here as is necessary to make clear the assumptions themselves. The ultimate justification for the point of view adopted must wait upon the results it yields in clarifying thinking, in stimulating cumulatively productive research, and finally in providing that groundwork of knowledge on which alone effective practical adjustments can be made.

The basic postulates regarding the nature of "reality" and "knowledge" upon which all science proceeds may be briefly stated as follows:

1. All data or experience with which man can become concerned consist of *the responses of the organisms-in-environment*. This includes the postulate of an external world and variations both in it and in the responders to it.[5]

2. Symbols, usually verbal, are invented to represent these responses.

3. These symbols are the immediate data of all communicable knowledge and therefore of all science.

4. All propositions or postulates regarding the more ultimate "realities" must always consist of inference, generalizations, or abstractions from these symbols and the responses which they represent.

5. These extrapolations are in turn represented symbolically, and we respond to them as we respond to other phenomena which evoke behavior.

C. Corollaries and Implications for Sociology

SOME OF THE COROLLARIES and implications of these postulates, especially as they affect present methods in the social sciences, need to be emphasized and elaborated briefly.

1. THE INFERENTIAL NATURE OF KNOWLEDGE AND "REALITY"

In the first place according to these postulates, all statements about the nature of the universe or any part of it are necessarily a verbalization of somebody's responses to *that which* evoked these responses. The nature of that which evoked them must always be an inference from the immediate datum, namely, our symbolized sensory experience.[6] All assertions about the *ultimate* "reality," "nature," "essence," or "being" of "things," or "objects" are therefore unverifiable hypotheses, and hence outside the sphere of science. Conversely, we assume that man and culture are definitely part of the cosmos. The *cosmos* is a word by which we designate the sum total of all the influences that precipitate responses in man. We assume further, that all phenomena of man and culture, in common with all nonhuman phenomena, are entirely contained within the cosmos and entirely dependent upon the energy transformations within that cosmos. We start with symbolized human responses as the immediate datum. As a metaphysical necessity we grant *that which* in the universe outside of the responding mechanism precipitates the response. After this is done, science is not concerned with the particular metaphysical hypotheses anyone may prefer to hold about the more ultimate nature of *that which* arouses responses.

2. WORDS AS OBJECTIVE PHENOMENA

It follows from the above that for scientific purposes all attempted distinctions, hypotheses, or assumptions regarding differences in the *ultimate* "nature" of so-called "physical" as contrasted with "social" data, between "material" and "immaterial," "mental," "spiritual," or "cultural" phenomena are ruled out. No relevant data (e.g., behavior designated by such words as "spiritual," etc.) are ruled out if they are manifest in human behavior of *any observable kind*. At present we shall attempt to deal only with the more objective of these behaviors. But since objectivity is here regarded *not as a characteristic of things but as those ways of responding which can be corroborated by others,*[7] it follows that the framework of science affords place for all known or knowable data. Of course, the less developed our objectifying technics are for certain experiences (i.e., the "subjective" and "spiritual") the greater is the task of communicating them so that they can be verified (the test of objectivity). Indeed, this process of objectifying them may involve analysis, reclassification, and designation by new and strange symbols. Many terms at present employed probably will be abandoned entirely as devoid of content when the behavior phenomena to which they once referred have been more adequately described by other terms. As science has advanced, this has been true of all pre-scientific terms and categories. In this connection we encounter one of the chief obstacles to the translation of subjective experience into objective data, i.e., communicating the former and rendering them verifiable. Let us take only one illustration.

In the opinion of the best chemists as recently as one hundred and fifty years ago, *phlogiston* was a necessary element in the explanation of combustion. The theory was that in all materials that burn there is present phlogiston, a substance without color, odor, taste, or weight. Even Priestley, to whom the discovery of oxygen is usually credited, continued to maintain during his lifetime the existence of phlogiston and the part it was supposed to play in combustion. By experiments involving much careful and accurate weighing, Lavoisier was able to demonstrate finally the unnecessary character of the hypothetical entity, phlogiston. Nevertheless, the older chemists of the day, thoroughly habituated to thinking about fire in terms of phlogiston continued to "feel" that the new explanation "left something out." It did leave something out, namely, a *word* to which the chemists of the day had become thoroughly habituated, and which was therefore as "real" to them as the word "wood" or whatever other words are used to symbolize the factors assumed to be present in a given fire. However, we do not contend that by abandoning phlogiston, modern chemists refuse to recognize a vital or relevant element in the explanation of fire.

Today, however, a considerable number of students of societal phenomena are still firmly convinced that the phenomena with which they have to deal cannot be adequately described or explained without, for example, a category called "mind," which carries with it a whole vocabulary of subsidiary terms (thought, experience, feeling, judgment, choice, will, value, emotion, etc., etc.) "We forget that these nouns are merely substitutes for verbs and go hunting for the things denoted by the nouns; but there are no such things; there are only the activities that we started with." [8] By this oversight, also, we avoid the necessity of defining operationally the behavior-units into which the phenomena of any field must be divided for scientific purposes. Any attempt to deal in other words with the behavior which these words are used to represent meets with the most determined resistance on the ground that *"something* has been left out." And what has been left out? Why, "will," "feeling," "ends," "motives," "values," etc. These are the phlogiston of the social sciences. Argument or demonstration that the behavior represented by these words is accorded full recognition within the present framework of the "physical" sciences are to some apparently as futile as were the arguments against phlogiston to Priestley. He *just knew* that any system which left out the word phlogiston was *ipso facto* fallacious. I have no doubt that a considerable part of the present content of the social sciences will turn out to be pure phlogiston. That fact will be discovered as soon as someone attempts operational definitions of the vocabulary which at present confounds these sciences. Yet, it is on the basis of such words that we undertake to set up a separate universe [9] to which the methods of inquiry recognized in the other ("physical") universe is held not to apply. The Germans properly designate this former field as that of the *Geisteswissenschaften*. The distinction between "science" and "social science" is, in fact, quite generally accepted as a matter of course. The present work continues, as a matter of necessity, to use the terminology here criticized because it is our purpose to communicate with the present generation. Also it is necessary to bring about the desired transition through the substitution of a new content for some of the old terms rather than abandoning them outright. Useless or undesirable words should be allowed to die as their content is taken over by new and more adequate terms. We contemplate a gradual transition to a dimensional and an operational terminology.

The following illustration from contemporary sociological literature further illustrates the tendency to regard familiar words as essential components of situations: "There is an essential difference, from the standpoint of causation, between a paper flying before the wind and a man flying from a pursuing crowd. The paper knows no fear and the wind no hate, but without fear and hate the man would not fly nor the crowd pursue. If we try to reduce fear to its bodily concomitants we merely substitute the concomitants for the reality experienced as fear. *We denude the world of meanings for the sake of a theory itself a false meaning which deprives us of all of the rest.*" [10] [Italics mine.]

Note the essential nature of the words *hate* and *fear* in this analysis. Even their translation into terms of their behavior-referents is alleged to "denude the world of meanings." Now if anyone wishes to interpret the flying of a paper before the wind in terms of hate and fear, as has doubtless frequently been done in ages past, I know of no way of refuting the analysis for it is determined by the terms, the framework, and the meanings adopted. *These categories* are not given in the phenomenon. Neither are the categories I should use in scientific description so given. In fact, I have no objection to the words "fear" and "hate" if they are defined in terms of physico-chemical, biolinguistic, or sociological behavior subject to objective verification. I have no doubt, either, that descriptions in these terms would vary widely in different cases of flying objects. For this reason, I do not declare MacIver's analysis of the man and the crowd as *false*. I merely point out that possibly I could analyze the situation in a frame of reference not involving the words "fear" or "hate" but in operationally defined terms of such character that all qualified observers would independently make the same analysis and predict the behavior under the given circumstances. Such a demonstration would not, of course, constitute an adequate substitute explanation to some people any more than Lavoisier's interpretation of fire was satisfactory to Priestley. Indeed, that interpretation is still meaningless to those not familiar with the framework and terminology of chemistry and physics. On the other hand, the principle of parsimony requires that we seek to bring into the same framework the explanation of all flying objects. In an animistic culture the imputation of fear to all flying objects (under the above circumstances) fulfills this requirement. Gradually, however, this explanation was abandoned for all inorganic phenomena, and more recently for the lower animals. The fear-hate categories are not generally used in describing or "explaining" the approach of the amoeba to its food although even the amoeba approaches food that can move away in a different way than it approaches food which has no power of locomotion.

The idea that the same general laws may be applicable to both "physical" and societal behavior may seem fantastic and inconceivable to many people. It is literally inconceivable to those who do not possess the symbolic technology in terms of which alone it can be conceived. For this reason, it may be that the next great developments in the social sciences will come not from professed social scientists but from people trained in other fields. The contributions of men like Comte, Ward, and Pareto, all of them technically trained in other sciences and in mathematics, are significant in this connection. In present day psychology, likewise, the major contributions are being made by men trained in engineering, physiology, and other "physical" sciences. This does not mean the contribution of social scientists will be worthless. They have performed and will perform valuable services in pointing out data, problems, and difficulties in their field. With much data already available, scientists with more adequate technical equipment will probably make the most important contributions to systematic sociology for some time to come. In the meantime, the general scientific and technical equipment of social scientists is, of course, rapidly improving.

The doctrine that man is the one unique object in the universe whose behavior cannot be explained within the framework found adequate for all others is, of course, a very ancient and respectable one. We merely make the contrary assumption in this work. From the latter point of view a paper flying before the wind is interpreted as the behavior of an object of *specified characteristics* reacting to a stimulus of *specified characteristics* within a specified field of force. Within this framework we describe the man and the crowd, the paper and the wind. The characteristics of these elements (and they may be specified to any degree desired including fully the "mental" aspects of some types of "flying", such as fear, hate, etc.) would never be the same in any two cases of wind and paper or of men and crowds. But it is the faith of science that sufficiently general principles can be found to cover all these situations, and that through these principles reliable predictions can be made of the probability of specific events.

3. THE RELATIVITY OF "EXISTENCE" AND "REALITY"

It will be observed that the above position regards "existence" and "reality" as always relative to some responding organism and that these words designate nothing absolute or final of the type usually implied by such words as "truth" and "fact." The only metaphysical position necessary and compatible with science is a postulate conceding the existence of *whatever* precipitates our responses, but making no further statements whatever about the absolute nature, characteristics or temporal-spatial qualities of these postulated entities. Phenomena exist for those organisms which respond to the stimuli in question but do not exist for organisms which do not so respond. If "wall" is defined as that which obstructs the movement of a person toward a given place, the existence of the wall is predicated upon that observed behavior of the person. To a micro-organism whose movement is in no way hindered by that which obstructs the person, the wall does not exist under the definition we have adopted. "Existence," "reality," the verb "is" as a mystical general designation, and a large number of similar words, and rules of logic constructed from them, are merely words designating behavior and behavior relationships. Apart from this behavior, the words are without content for science.

The deep-seated nature of these language habits and the rules of logic couched in these terms cause many people to feel that the bottom drops out of all "sensible" discourse unless *certain* things (as

contrasted with the mere postulate of *something*) can be declared to
exist quite irrespective of anybody's responses to them. If this position is assumed, it follows that *someone must declare what things do
so exist.* In spite of the mischief and obscurantism which has resulted
from this position throughout history, contemporary scientists, and
especially social scientists, are still inclined to cling to some "eternal
verities" specified or implicitly taken for granted by themselves.
They still undertake to discard new theories precisely on the same
ground as did certain contemporaries of Galileo, namely, the conflict
of these theories with "ultimate realities." [11] The latter are assumed
to be given in nature and self-evident to all decent and competent
persons. We are usually so thoroughly habituated to the "ultimate
realities" as to be unaware of the origin of these word-habits and
impatient of any inquiry into that subject. The most vigorous critics
of *past* obscurantists are likely to be also the most passionate defenders of the current faith. Did not their present beliefs triumph
over "Falsehood," "Error," "Superstition," etc., and does not this
sufficiently establish the former as "Truth" now finally "discovered"?
Because of their mistaken notion that these words are absolute *entities* of some sort instead of an organism's designation of certain
types of responses entirely relative to itself, they follow precisely in the
footsteps of the popes and the priests for whom they profess such
contempt.

Scientists had better confine themselves to a modest postulate of
"x" which precipitates our responses and the nature of which we
tentatively infer from these responses. The justification of even the
postulate of the *"x"* had better be its demonstrable efficiency in
helping us comprehend our world rather than in vociferous declarations about its "existence" and its "truth." Then if, for example, the
time ever comes when the data of experience are more adequately
comprehended by the assumption of a round rather than an elliptical
orbit of the earth or any other modification in even the most widely
accepted viewpoints, we can with full freedom and consistency adopt
such a view.

Informed scientists in other fields have, of course, accepted this
view of even their most stable formulations. Einstein and Infeld
have expressed the viewpoint with admirable clarity in the following
passage:

"In our endeavor to understand reality we are somewhat like a man trying to understand the mechanism of a closed watch. He sees the face and the moving hands, even hears its ticking, but he has no way of opening the case. If he is ingenious he may form some picture of a mechanism which could be responsible for all the things he observes, but he may never be quite sure his picture is the only one which could explain his observations. *He will never be able to compare his picture with the real mechanism and he cannot even imagine the possibility or the meaning of such a comparison.* But he certainly believes that, as his knowledge increases, his picture of reality will become simpler and simpler and will explain a wider and wider range of his sensuous impressions. He may also believe in the existence of the ideal limit of knowledge and that it is approached by the human mind. He may call this ideal limit the objective truth." [12] [Italics mine.]

The same authors have also recognized a point too frequently overlooked by those who believe that past theories were merely a morass of error serving no purpose but to obscure the truth now so happily finally attained. Say Einstein and Infeld: "The new theory shows the merits as well as the limitations of the old theory and allows us to regain our old concepts from a higher level. This is true not only for the theories of electric fluids and field, but for all changes in physical theories, however revolutionary they may seem.... To use a comparison, we could say that creating a new theory is not like destroying an old barn and erecting a skyscraper in its place. It is rather like climbing a mountain, gaining new and wider views, discovering unexpected connections between our starting point and its rich environment. But the point from which we started out still exists and can be seen, although it appears smaller and forms a tiny part of our broad view gained by the mastery of the obstacles on our adventurous way up." [13]

The above reasoning applies with equal validity to our most firmly established orientations and to our more transient theories. It is not likely that we shall have to revise our notion of the earth's shape. But it is highly likely that we shall have to abandon or thoroughly revise some of our most profoundly held notions about man and human society. The resistance which behaviorism encountered some years ago in psychology and sociology even in some scienitfic circles suggests that science had better make no absolute and final declarations about "existence," "reality," and "truth," in any field. Sociology

especially had better keep clear of such declarations. It is quite common for researchers in sociology to be told that however rigorous has
been their devotion to all the requirements of scientific method, their
results unfortunately do not square with "the very nature of the
thing" studied; its "true or real content" has been missed, and so
forth.[14] The mere objectivity of findings in the sense of corroboration
by other workers is not enough from the point of view I am attacking. The findings must also, and primarily, square with some "objective reality" (represented only by certain words) which is declared to
"exist" independently of anybody's observations or corroboration.

Fortunately, scientists are likely to go about their business without
too much attention to these strictures. They record their observations,
analyze and synthesize them according to rules that experience has
shown yield a certain kind of result. If, when they are through, it
seems more sensible to say the earth is round rather than flat, they
say so, suffer persecutions, but go on their way. They have done it
in the past, and will doubtless do it in the future, even when it
does to "the very nature" of man and society what Darwinism did.
I have taken here an epistemological position compatible with such
developments.

4. THE VISIBILITY AND OBJECTIVITY OF SOCIETAL PHENOMENA

Within our universe of discourse, then, all data are known to us
only through human responses and we infer both the existence and
the characteristics of any phenomena from these responses. A taboo,
a custom, an "idea," or a belief is, therefore, as a datum, as "tangible," "real," observable, measurable, and otherwise susceptible of
scientific study as is a stone, a table, or a horse. The contrary assumption flows from the fact that the responses aroused through certain
senses, notably of touch and sight, being responses for which the most
highly developed objective symbols have been invented, are therefore
assumed to possess a "tangibility" which events that have not yet been
thus symbolized do not have. Now the words "tangibility," "reality,"
etc., may be used profitably to describe a degree of objectification
of our responses to some data while such terms as "intangible,"
"spiritual," "nonmaterial," describe a lesser degree of objectivity of
responses. But these terms cannot be used to indicate intrinsic characteristics of data in the present frame of reference. The alleged
greater "tangibility" of certain "physical" events resides not in the

events, but in our more highly objectified methods of responding to them. *That response* which we call custom, affection, pain, anger, the welfare of our grandchildren, the Future Life, or what not, consists of reactions of sense receptors to stimuli from outside or inside the organism as truly as our experience of a stone or a tree.

This point is fundamental and must be taken quite literally if we really contemplate bringing societal phenomena within the framework of natural science. We must be able to show that symbols such as honor, duty, loyalty, etc., and the behavior which they represent are as observable and objective data as are baseball, the seasonal flight of birds, or the jump of an electric spark. "Baseball," "flight," and "spark" are words by which one person communicates to another certain of his responses to whatever phenomena precipitate these responses. Honor, duty, and loyalty are another group of such words designating people's responses to other phenomena. The capacity of a word or any other stimulus to evoke a given response depends upon our conditioning, at some time in our existence as an organism, to respond in a given way in a given stimulus-response situation. All of these words stand for behavior of some sort. To the extent that numbers of individuals use the same word to designate similar behavior phenomena (i.e., to the extent that numbers of individuals behave in a given way in a given situation) it is conventional to designate the phenomena to which they respond as objective. Phenomena are objective in science to the extent that this criterion of agreement, corroboration, or verifiability is satisfied.

Failure to grasp this relativistic meaning of objectivity is perhaps the basic reason for fundamental misunderstandings in the social sciences. The common objection to the position advanced in this book, usually designated as behavioristic or positivistic, is that it cannot, it is said, take account of what men feel or think.[15] In elaboration of this statement Cooley's "bold statement that the solid facts of social life are the facts of the imagination" is quoted.[16] "My friend is best defined," it is said, "as what I imagine he will do and say to me on occasion"—a surprisingly behavioristic statement. The point is further illustrated by the statement that "when John and Tom meet there are six persons present. There is John's real self (known only to his Maker) [sic], John's idea of himself, and John's idea of Tom, and, of course, three corresponding Toms. Cooley goes on to say that there are really twelve or more, including John's idea of Tom's idea of John's idea of Tom. In these 'echoes of echoes of echoes' of personality we have an *a fortiori* consideration of the importance of *the subjective aspect of conduct*." [17] [Italics mine.]

If it is assumed that any social scientist, behaviorist or other, proposes to ignore any or all of the above data, it is not surprising that the thought has caused considerable agitation. No supporter of such a view is ever cited by the critics, and I have never in the course of a considerable survey of the literature encountered an exponent of the position. The better known authorities, including the most extreme behaviorists, have specifically disavowed any such view.[18] Not only have the behaviorists apparently failed to communicate what their position is, but they have succeeded in arousing in their critics nightmares of vast proportions. The obvious fact is that communication has broken down on this subject. Whether the fault lies at the sending or the receiving end is not immediately relevant. The important thing is to clarify the position if possible, since the possibility of objective study of phenomena of the kind illustrated above is obviously basic to a science of sociology.

I hold that "echoes" and "shadows" are just as truly physical phenomena subject to objective scientific study as are the phenomena which shadows and echoes reflect. The charge that we propose to ignore the phenomena of "imagination," "thought," or "consciousness" is as unwarranted as would be a similar charge that physicists deny the phenomena of shadows and echoes. The physicist demands verifiable sensory evidence of echoes and shadows exactly as he does of original noises that echo or of objects that cast shadows. The sociologist must similarly demand sensory evidence of the imaginings, thoughts, and other phenomena of "consciousness." When he has such evidence he is as much interested in the phenomena of what men think and feel as in any other data. Imaginings, thoughts, and feelings manifest themselves if at all through symbolic or other neuro-muscular behavior. As such they are as proper subject for scientific study as are all other phenomena. This holds for all so-called introspective phenomena as well as for phenomena assumed to originate outside of the observer. (Actually, of course, all *responses* are "subjective" or "introspective" in the sense that the response occurs before it is communicated.)

The assumed inaccessibility of the data of consciousness to objective study arises from the undeveloped state of the technic for such study.[19] No behaviorist questions the scientific validity of a physician taking his own temperature, pulse count, or recording by any method subject to verification, his observation of the behavior of any part of his organism in relation to stimuli of whatever kind, societal or "physical." It is a problem of developing an objective terminology and instruments with which to observe and describe experience which is now very inadequately communicable or subject to verification. "The possibility of one man's observing another's mental processes, like the possibility of observing another's digestion becomes a question of developing laboratory technique." [20] This technic need not contemplate substituting our experience for his directly. Like all other knowledge it is usually inferred from objective signs. In short, it is only a matter of what degree of objectivity we shall require before we can use them as a basis for scientific generalizations. Of course, we are using and should continue in the meantime to use these data for all they are worth in their present form.

The same reasoning holds for the common assumption that a strictly behavioristic description of societal behavior denies "the relevance of anticipated social ends as a partial determinant of social action." [21] Anticipated ends, in the sense of "conscious" prevision, whenever they become stimuli to action, exist as words or other symbols to which the organism responds as it does to other stimuli. The same is true of memories, "values," "meanings," "ideals," "ideas," and all the rest of the phenomena which are alleged to be unapproachable by the accepted methods of science. Again, the error lies in assuming that the telic character or purposiveness which we like to attribute to societal behavior is an intrinsic character of the behavior rather than our way of describing it. All phenomena *may* be described in teleological, theological, or magical terms. We have merely abandoned the practice of ascribing "malice" to the tree which falls "in order to" block our path, or of attributing "planning" to the amoeba in approaching its food.

Physicists have likewise lost interest in the question of whether an echo or a shadow is "objective," "real," or "exists." The investigation and description of an "echo of an echo of an echo" proceeds according to the same principles as the investigation and description of any other noise. When we adopt this attitude toward the "intangibles" which so bedevil and frustrate contemporary sociological theory, we shall presently find that certain metaphysical questions of "existence," "reality," "subjectivity," and "tangibility" can take their place with the question of how many angels can stand on the point of a needle and other profound issues that agitated learned men of other ages.

Full inquiry into the conditions affecting the observed behavior is required in any case. If it is desired to designate a certain type of conditions common among human beings by the term "malice," there is no objection to doing so. It is the use of the word as a substitute for the investigation of the conditions that is here under criticism. As convenient classifications of types of data there is, likewise, no objection to designating some as "physical" and "material" and others as "cultural," "social," or even "spiritual," provided we do not make assumptions that these classifications affect the method by which we know the phenomena in question, i.e., through sensory responses of some kind. It is true that both an iron fence and a taboo will keep men from touching an object or going to a certain place. It is also true that the taboo will have this effect only upon the behavior of men conditioned to a certain culture, while the fence may have the same effect on all men. Therefore, by men in general, greater objectivity is ascribed properly to the fence. But *to the men conditioned by the given culture,* the taboo has the same degree of objectivity, the test of objectivity in either case being the observed behavior of the men. From this behavior of the men, the existence, meaning, objectivity, and other characteristics of both fence and taboo is inferred. Obviously, the fact that we ascribe equal degrees of objectivity to two things for given groups of men does not mean that we claim they are the "same," "alike," or "similar" in any or all *other* respects. The fact to keep in mind is that all existence, data, reality, or being is relative to some observer and, of course, to his frame of reference. Obviously, to some of the lower animals with different sensory apparatus and background of experiences, many data sensed by all men do not exist and *vice versa.* Likewise, different men sense different things. Things which all or nearly all men respond to in very much the same way, i.e., an iron fence, we call relatively objective, physical, material, tangible, etc. Things to which only relatively few, or only one, respond in the same way without special cultural conditioning are termed subjective, intangible, spiritual, etc. We are not contending that the data called intangible and spiritual today may not be properly so described. We merely point out wherein their intangibility resides, so that, if we develop response technics which permit the checking and corroboration of the responses to things today called intangible, they would then be tangible. Whether this can ever be done to some "subjective" data remains to be seen. In any case we are more likely to make progress in this quest if we assume as a working hypothesis that it can be done. We have no choice but to proceed on that hypothesis if we wish to bring these data within the domain of science.

5. MEANING AS A TYPE OF CLASSIFICATION

Much of the difficulty which the above position seems to involve is the result of a failure to recognize that within the framework here advanced, words themselves, spoken or written, are just as truly entities to which we respond as all other objects are. Under other orientations, words are frequently unique and mysterious, not to say magical, entities, because it is alleged, we respond to their *meanings* rather than to the words as objects or as "physical" stimuli. This is a confusion flowing from the assumptions dealt with under our first postulate. Our response to a stone is also to its meaning to us, i.e., the conditioning we have undergone to the word "stone." Prior to such conditioning it has no "meaning" to us (in the sense of knowledge) and calls for no response as a symbol. All words (stone as well as taboo) are symbolic designations of some behavior phenomenon to which we respond. It is our response which gives it "meaning." [22] The meaning of anything we respond to at all is implicit in the response and part of it. We do not respond symbolically to that which has *no* meaning to us. Meaningless things, words, or symbols are a contradiction in terms; the very fact that we call them meaningless proves that they have *that* meaning, i.e., we so classify them. We use the expression to designate, of course, phenomena that do not fit in consistently with the frame of reference in which we try to place them. A "nonsense" syllable, for example, has meaning *as such*. What we mean when we call it meaningless is that it does not have *a certain kind* of meaning that other syllables in a given language have.

To say that a statement is meaningless is obviously as meaningful a statement as any other. Only *words* or *statements* (symbols) about the world (not objects *per se* which are only inferences from responses) can have meaning. We encounter here the old question as to whether we can "think" without symbols. This question can be resolved only by an arbitrary definition of "thinking." Since all responses that have any scientific import involve symbolic systems, we take the generally accepted view that all thinking involves symbols and that only when symbolized do "objects" or behavior have meaning.

6. CATEGORIES AS GENERALIZED HABITS

What has been said above about words in general also applies to categories and classifications of phenomena. The limitations of man's sense organs permit him to respond only to certain aspects of the whole universe (i.e., everything that might be responded to) at any one time. We mean by an "aspect," "segment," "field," or "part," any situation to which our neural organization allows us to respond as a unit while responding in a secondary way to the relation of this situation to a larger situation in which the former is considered as encompassed. The problems that confront us at a given time define and evoke selective responses. We designate them as parts or wholes according to their individual sufficiency for the adjustment-needs of the occasion. On this basis, we designate some situations as "wholes" and others as "parts." It follows, of course, that what is regarded as a "whole" with reference to one situation may be regarded as a "part" with reference to another, and *vice versa*. Thus a cell may be a whole and the solar system a part, according to the frame of reference adopted. The words are therefore merely designations of types of response, not intrinsic qualities or characteristics of objects or situations as is implied by some writers on "Gestalt" psychology.[23] In other words, all aspects, segments, parts, or other categories or classifications, including the classification of the sciences, are defined by whatever behavior the organism finds relevant to its adjustment needs (including the intellectual needs of a given organism at a given time) to restore that balance the disturbance of which we postulate as the occasion for any or all behavior. The lines of classification which we impose upon phenomena "are not walls of separation, but more like the parallels and meridians of the globe, which in no way mar its continuity but make our sphere intelligible and comprehensible from our various points of view." [24]

The number of different aspects of the universe to which it is possible for the human organism to respond probably are practically unlimited. The permutations and combinations possible among such a multiplicity of factors as those to which the human senses are sensitive, as well as the constantly appearing new aspects resulting from the phenomena of evolution or change in man himself, his technology, and his environment make the social universe alone a field within which an almost unlimited number of classifications of phenomena (selective responses) are possible.

The broadest and most general classification of aspects of the universe which any species will make consists of those aspects which involve the adjustment needs of all or nearly all individuals. The broad divisions of the universe introduced by some of the ancients such as earth, air, fire, water; man, as distinct from other animals; distinctions between body, soul, and mind, etc., represent designations of aspects of the universe calling for special types of responses to which practically all people were called upon to make common-sense adjustments of certain fairly uniform kinds. For example, it is found that changing one's position from point to point by walking is under given conditions always possible on land but not on water. Air, likewise, is an aspect of the universe to which all are compelled to make specific responses different from those adapted to locomotion on land and water. The constant verification of these responses by everyone, permits universal assent to the imputation of certain characteristics to each of these aspects of man's environment. This is how *all* phenomena come to have attributed to them their generally recognized characteristics. That is, we assign to *that which* arouses *certain responses, words designating the qualities or characteristics which differentiate these responses from other responses.* Earth is that which supports us when we walk, water is that which does not support us if we try to walk on it but which is definable in terms of our *other* responses to it, etc.

We delimit the total universe, therefore, into aspects, categories, and classifications on the basis of the differential responses with which we are compelled to adjust. These adjustments consist, of course, of observably different behaviors. In the human species, these different behaviors are represented by different words. To these aspects of the universe to which nearly all men respond in nearly the same way we attribute high objectivity, "reality," "existence," "being," etc. This is the basis of "common sense," the experiential precursor of science. There are other aspects with reference to which the uniformity of response is not so easily observable or verifiable and for which the descriptive symbols are not as yet so easily checkable against the behavior for which they are alleged to stand. To these aspects we therefore attribute lesser objectivity, lesser "reality," etc. The point to be observed is that the *divisions, categories, classifications,* and *groupings* of the phenomena of the universe are *words representing* differential *responses of man.* The objectivity of any aspect of the universe (situation) as contrasted with another, therefore, depends upon its capacity to evoke uniform responses from large numbers of people.[25] Since the overwhelming majority of these responses in the human species become known to others only through verbal behavior, the objectivity of phenomena depend largely upon the possibility of communicating accurately the meaning of words so as to insure that a given person uses a given word to represent the same kind of experience that other people use the word to represent. This we achieve chiefly through specifying in terms already highly objectified, and ultimately in overt behavior of some sort, such as pointing to an object, or going through the *operations* which we use the new term to designate.

It is quite essential to remember this basic nature of all categories in order to avoid becoming involved in insoluble metaphysical questions of ultimate reality, as we have pointed out above, and in order not to create the impression that the various classifications of human groupings represent anything more ultimate than ways of responding to aspects of the universe to which adjustment of some sort is made. On the scientific level that adjustment consists chiefly of the need of scientists to relieve the intellectual tension which comes of inability to fit certain phenomena into a coherent framework so that their curiosity can come to rest.

The postulates, axioms, and assumptions, and the corollaries we draw from them, constitute a symbolic frame of reference or universe of discourse, the origin and properties of which will be further discussed in Chapter 3. No orderly discussion is possible without such a framework for it is only by reference to some such framework that individual statements about phenomena have meaning. Since the elementary rules of grammar of any language constitute the most general of such frameworks, we usually take the reference for granted and do not state postulates explicitly. As a result we assume too lightly that the knowledge regarding which we have developed familiar verifying technics has an inherency in the universe, instead of being only a more uniform way of responding. In short, frames of reference and universes of discourse are themselves merely comprehensive ways of responding to large configurations of data. "Both mathematics and scientific theories," says Bell, "are nothing more immortal than convenient man-made maps for the correlation of human experiences." [26] We here make the same statement about any and all theories and generalizations whatsoever. Their "truth" or validity will rest on the same practical test upon which we estimate the adequacy of any other response, namely, whether it achieves the adjustment sought.

7. THE UTILITARIAN TEST OF ALL THOUGHT-SYSTEMS

The above orientation calls for no theoretical argument, therefore, as to the "truth" of our system as against theological and philosophical terms and postulates *within their own system*. Many theologies are quite as logical, comprehensive, and self-sufficient theoretical systems as is science. Thus the postulate of an omnipresent, omniscient, and just God, or of a devil directing the affairs of the universe, provides a frame into which events may be fitted according to certain general rules of logic, i.e., of verbal syntax. The postulate of the earth as a flat body around which the sun and the other planets move is another frame of reference into which common-sense observations may be fitted logically. The postulate of a round earth moving around the sun is an alternative frame of reference. The only legitimate criterion for judging frames of reference, as such, is the degree to which they are consistent with themselves. From the standpoint of the use of a given frame as a chart or compass for practical adjustments, the criterion becomes, of course, its practical adequacy, i.e., its usefulness in securing the desired adjustment. By the first criterion several widely disparate systems may be equally defensible. By the second criterion, one system will, under given circumstances, tend to be superior (on the ground noted) to others. These two criteria must not be confused. Under the first criterion the postulates of the present work should be judged by their self-consistency, the possibility of logically deducing from them theorems capable of empirical verification, and their compatibility with the general framework of science. Under the second criterion they must be judged by their simplicity, their generality, and by their capacity to provide a basis for practical adjustments.

The futile scholastic discussion of many subjects especially affecting man and the social order owe their futility to the failure to designate explicitly the frame of reference, the postulates, and the rules upon which the discussion proceeds. This failure is in turn due to the common assumption that frames of reference are in some way inherent in the universe instead of being pure constructions for our convenience—"ways of looking at things."

The conditions under which men live, including their cultural heritage determines, of course, in a broad way what frames of reference will be invented at any given time. The point of view here presented, for example, is the result of the tension which comes of trying to live in an intellectual world which is half scientific and half something else. Although the thought pattern of science is bearing down on us from every side, we nevertheless try to avoid its full implications in the sociological realm on the ground that the latter involve "mental" or "spiritual" factors. Out of these factors it is attempted to erect a separate order of being or of knowledge called *Geisteswissenschaft*. In the meantime, the incompatibility of the assumptions behind such a view in the light of increasing psychological knowledge about the nature of the "mental" categories, is destroying the basis for the distinction.

Since failure to recognize the essential nature of propositions, postulates, and frames of reference as discussed above results in the most widespread and fundamental misunderstandings and futile arguments, these essential points cannot be too strongly emphasized. It must be admitted too that scientists as well as their opponents frequently overlook these considerations. The tirades against religion, theology, and other systems of thought by erstwhile adherents to these faiths who have recently discovered "science" are often evidence of a mistaken notion regarding the nature of both science and the faiths of the fathers. *All* of these systems are merely adjustment technics which have been found more or less satisfactory to their adherents *under given conditions* at different times. As times and conditions change, all of these frames of reference, including present science, may be expected to prove inadequate, and be abandoned for radically different postulates, and may proceed perhaps, according to different technics and systems of logic.

The tests of the adequacy ("truth") of any system at any given time will in any event be determined by certain empirical tests, notably whether the system affords a rationale of the adjustments that have to be made and whether it aids in planning those adjustments. The vogue of "physical" science today springs from just such demonstrable relevance in an industrial, mechanical age in which adjustments to remote environments have become necessary through developed means of communication. The same conditions have, of course, forced the "social" sciences in the same direction and will ultimately, I think, compel them to align themselves completely with the "physical." But it is impossible to show that the orientations of science have any greater (or as great) relevance to the practical adjustments of life in a convent or a monastery (and some of the present academic counterparts of these societies) than theology. Different ways of life demand different ways of thought. In abandoning here a traditional distinction between the "physical" and the "social," "mental," and "spiritual" we are not doing so under the delusion of having "discovered" "new," "absolute" truth. Neither do we deny, ignore, or abolish any phenomena whatsoever. Philosophies may themselves be considered sociologically as systems of verbal behavior, but their declared objectives and objects (entities allegedly represented by the words employed) need not be considered in a scientific framework unless the phenomena designated by the words used can be verified. We aim merely to discuss from a certain explicit point of view the *same* behavior phenomena with which all other sociological systems (including all the theologies and social philosophies) deal, and to organize them as far as possible according to the general pattern of science. The "truth," the merits, or the advantages of this point of view will have to be determined by the same practical usefulness which has given modern science in other fields its prestige and its following as against the thoughtways it has supplanted.

8. THE NONETHICAL NATURE OF SCIENCE

It should be clear from the above that it is the primary function of all science to formulate the sequences that are observable in *any* phenomena in order to be able to predict their recurrence. I shall specify in a later chapter what I consider to be the particular field of sociology. In the meantime, it is desirable to point out, as another corollary of the position stated above, that questions of ethics or of what "ought to be" must not in science be confused with what observations indicate. Nor must sociological problems be confused with "social" problems in the sense of adjustments deemed desirable by anyone in any time, place, or circumstance. The prevention of crime is a social problem. The relationship between criminality and population density or any other social condition is a sociological problem. Sociological and all other scientific questions have to do with the formulation of verifiable relationships. Social questions have to do with other and more general readjustments of social conditions with reference to any goals toward which man may aspire.

The fact that there is a relationship between these fields is no reason for confusing them. It is entirely permissible for society to maintain educational institutions and courses to transmit to the young a knowledge of past and current social events from the viewpoint of the dominant ethical and social system that prevails or which is idealized at any given time. Orientation courses, courses in reform, ethics, idealism, religion, current events, and social work are doubtless a useful and necessary part of the educational program of contemporary society. If it is found administratively convenient or otherwise advisable to give this instruction in departments of sociology and by "sociologists" that is again a practical question of educational administration. To confuse such subject matter with scientific problems, however, is mere confusion and cannot lead to the solution of scientific problems. If we give little attention to traditional "social" problems in the present work it is not because we are not personally interested in these problems as all members of human society are likely to be, but because we do not wish to confuse them with certain *other* problems with which we wish to concern ourselves.

As we shall see later, the approach to societal phenomena here proposed provides a place for all societal data whatsoever including those conventionally designated as ethical, idealistic, spiritual, or esthetic. It does not follow that we must adopt the conventional categories in terms of which these phenomena are treated in other systems. Only *the behavior designated by these conventional categories* are entitled to recognition. Much confusion results from overlooking the fact that no theory legitimately can be required to adopt the *categories* of another theory. Take, for example, the constant demand upon thoroughgoing social scientists as to how they propose within their frame of reference to deal with "spiritual" data—what about "values," "ideals," "ethics," the good, the true, and the beautiful? Frightened by the prestige of the source from which these

inquiries frequently come, the sociologist, himself often a bit worrie
over his own heterodoxy, makes ludicrous attempts to provide withi
a scientific framework place for *categories* which have no place i
that framework any more than scientific categories have a place in
theological framework. It is not necessary for a priest to give a
account of the cellular structure of the Holy Ghost. The only answe
which a scientist needs to give to the question as to how "spiritua
data are to be handled within the scientific framework is to point o
that all the *observable behavior* covered by this category is readi
and fully provided for in the scientific framework. The *category itse*
clearly does not have to be, and should not be, incorporated, an
more than the categories of science can or need be incorporated int
theology.

The root of this difficulty lies, of course, in the naive conceit of ma
which induces him to believe that any word which he may inver
inevitably has a necessary counterpart in nature or in supernatur;
regions. Nowhere does this confusion become more evident than i
discussions of the relationship of ethics and values to the social sc
ences. As we have already pointed out in another connection, th
confusion arises from converting the verb "valuating," meaning an
discriminatory or selective behavior, into a noun called "values." W
then go hunting for the *things* denoted by this noun. But there ar
no such things. There are only the valuating *activities* we starte
with. What was said above about motives applies with equal force t
values. They are clearly inferences from behavior. That is, we say
thing *has* value or *is* a value when people behave toward it so as t
retain or increase their possession of it. It may be economic good
and services, political office, a mate, graduation, prestige, a clea
conscience, or anything you please. Since valuations or values ar
empirically observable patterns of behavior, they may be studied a
such, by the same general techniques we use to study other behavior

As a matter of fact, everybody is more or less regularly engage
in such study of other people's values. It is quite essential to any kin
of satisfactory living in any community. We try to find out as soon a
possible what the values of our neighbors are. How do we find out
We observe their behavior, including their verbal behavior. We lister
to what other people say about them, we notice what they spend
their money for, how they vote, whether they go to church, and a
hundred other things. On a more formal and scientific level, opinion

polls on men and issues are taken to reflect the values of large groups. Economists, of course, have been studying for years certain kinds of evaluations of men through the medium of prices.

There appears to be no reason why values should not be studied as objectively as any other phenomena, for they are an inseparable part of behavior. The conditions under which certain values arise, i.e., the conditions under which certain kinds of valuating behavior take place, and the effects of "the existence of certain values" (as we say) in given situations are precisely what the social sciences must study and what they are studying. These values or valuating behaviors, like all other behavior, are to be observed, classified, interpreted, and generalized by the accepted techniques of scientific procedure.

Why, then, is the value problem considered unique and insurmountable in the social sciences?

The main reason seems to be that social scientists, like other people, often have strong feelings about religion, art, politics, and economics. That is, they have their likes and dislikes in these matters as they have in wine, women, and song. As a result of these preferences, both physical and social scientists frequently join other citizens to form pressure groups to advance the things they favor, including their own economic or professional advancement, Labor, Capital, Democracy, the True Church, or what not. To do so is the right of every citizen, and there is no canon of science or of civil law which requires scientists to abjure the rights which are enjoyed by all other members of a community.

The confusion about values seems to have arisen because both scientists and the public have frequently assumed that, when scientists engage in ordinary pressure-group activity, that activity somehow becomes science or scientific activity. This is a most mischievous fallacy. It is not surprising, perhaps, that the public should be confused on this point, because it may not always be clear when a scientist is expressing a scientific conclusion and when he is expressing a personal preference. But it is unpardonable for scientists themselves to be confused about what they know and say in their capacity as scientists and what they favor in religion, morals, and public policy. To pose as disinterested scientists announcing scientific conclusions when in fact they are merely expressing personal preferences is simple fraud, no matter how laudable or socially desirable may be the scientists' "motives" and objectives.

But is it possible for a person to play two or more distinct roles, such as scientist and citizen, without confusing the two? The answer is that it is being done every day. It is the most obvious commonplace that the actress who plays Juliet in the afternoon and Lady Macbeth at night does not allow her moral or other preference for one of these roles to influence her performance of the other. In any event, her competence is measured by her ability to play each role convincingly. During the same day she may also be expected to fulfill the roles of wife, mother, etc. Likewise, the chemist who vigorously campaigns against the use of certain gases in war obviously cannot allow that attitude to influence in the slightest degree the methods of producing or analyzing these gases. Science, as such, is non-moral. There is nothing in scientific work, as such, which dictates to what ends the products of science shall be used.

In short, it is not true that "to understand and describe a system involving values is impossible without some judgment of values." I can certainly report and understand the bald fact that a certain tribe kills its aged and eats them, without saying one word about the goodness or badness of that practice according to my own standards, or allowing these standards of mine to prevent me from giving an accurate report of the facts mentioned. The only value judgments which any properly trained scientist makes about his data are judgments regarding their relevance to his problem, the weight to be assigned to each aspect, and the general interpretation to be made of the observed events. These are problems which no scientist can escape, and they are not at all unique or insuperable in the social sciences.

Have scientists, then, no special function or obligation in determining the ends for which scientific knowledge is to be used? As scientists, *it is their business to determine reliably the immediate and remote costs and consequences of alternate possible courses of action, and to make these known to the public.* Scientists may then *in their capacity as citizens* join with others in advocating one alternative rather than another, as they prefer.

There appears to be a good deal of misunderstanding of my position as stated in the preceding paragraph. Many earnest scientists as well as literary men seem to feel that my distinction between the scientist, as scientist, and the scientist, as citizen, is somehow invalid or misleading. Thus C. P. Snow points out that the scientist, by virtue of possessing certain knowledge, thereby becomes saddled with "a direct and personal responsibility. It is not enough to say that scientists have a responsibility as citizens. They have a much greater one than that [?], and one different in kind [?]. For scientists have a moral imperative to say what they know." (Brackets mine.) [27]

I certainly agree that scientists have this moral imperative—*both* in their capacity as scientists and in their capacity as citizens. It is one of the requirements of science for the scientist to publish his results and how they were reached. The implication that nonscientists do not have this responsibility, this moral imperative, seems to me untenable. *Both* the scientist and the nonscientist *in their capacity as citizens* have a "moral imperative" "to say what they know" if they happen to know that a time bomb is ticking away under the city hall or that the water supply is being subtly poisoned. It seems absurd to me to say that the scientist also *in his capacity as scientist* has a moral imperative to prevent the city hall from being blown up. The question of whether or not to blow up the city hall is not a scientific question, and it is not the type of question which any science, and least of all, physics, can answer. To say what one knows may involve costs and consequences of the most serious kind, but these are consequences to which both scientist and nonscientist are subject. Fortunately, as Snow has pointed out, scientists perhaps have at least as much moral stamina as nonscientists in such matters. Thus we escape the greater disasters to which we might otherwise be exposed.

An illustration may clarify the point. In the report of the hearings of a U.S. Senate Committee on the bill establishing the National Science Foundation there occurs this item:

Senator Fulbright: I asked an able scientist yesterday if he would define social science. I had been worrying about that. He said in his definition, "In the first place, I would not call it science. What is commonly called social science is one individual or group of individuals telling another group how they should live." [28]

As is well known, this is a very generally accepted view and, unfortunately, perhaps in large part a warranted view. My point is that it is not *necessarily* true, and that one aim of all social scientists should be to make it always *false*. If so, social scientists should first agree that the sole function of scientific work is *to grind out and publish systematically related and significant "if. . . then" propositions which are demonstrably probable to a certain degree under given circumstances.* Under this definition "to say what one knows," i.e., *to publish one's findings* is certainly a clear imperative. Any advocacy or attempt on the part of a scientist, in his capacity of *scientist,* to specify what scientific knowledge is to be used for is equally clearly outside the scientific sphere as defined. *In his capacity as citizen,* the scientist may of course advocate anything his heart desires with all the passion and resources at his command. If we do not rigorously insist on this distinction between scientific knowledge as contrasted with all other forms of knowledge whatsoever, we invite the corruption of science by injecting into it the biases of human preferences, tastes, and values which is precisely the charge today laid at the door of the social sciences.

Many sincere and thoughtful people, while agreeing for the most part with the position advanced above, nevertheless hesitate at some of its implications. The question takes this form: Presumably the ideal scientist, in his role as scientist, has allegiance to only one belief, namely, that the presently developing methods of modern scientific inquiry are more likely than any other methods to yield useful warranted assertions for the guidance of men in society. Does it not follow that such a scientist, in his role as such, should advocate whatever form of government proves most favorable and least obstructive or inhibitive to such inquiry?

There can be no doubt, it seems to me, that if my definition of scientific method is accepted, my answer to the question must be an unqualified negative. I agree that a scientist, in his capacity as such, might find that *if the criteria* of governments more and less favorable to the advancement of science are specified, it is possible for the scientist strictly in his capacity as scientist to say that Government A is preferable to Government B, because the criteria now are the "if" in an "if ... then" proposition. The mores of science require him to publish this finding, *including the criteria.* I know of no canon or science which requires *or permits* him *as a scientist* to *advocate* the form of government which according to the stipulated criteria is "best" for the advancement of science. But I think it is both his right and his duty *as a citizen* not only to publish his finding (which is required also by the mores of science) but to advocate that form of government. The crucial point is that the scientific conclusions *depend upon the criteria.* And *the criteria* were not arrived at by scientific procedures. They were *taken,* as they always must be—they are the *"if"* in all scientific conclusions. And all scientific conclusions involve and include the *"if." All* scientific generalizations hold only under stipulated conditions. *No* scientific laws *in any science* hold *except* under stipulated conditions.

To the extent that their reputation and prestige is great, and to the extent that their tastes are shared by the masses of men, scientists will, of course, be influential in causing others to accept the goals the scientists recommend. In this sense, social science will doubtless become, as physical science already is, an important influence in determining the wants of men. That is, as a result of scientific knowledge, men will not want impossible or mutually exclusive things. They will not seek to increase foreign trade and at the same time establish more comprehensive and higher tariffs. They will not seek to reduce crime but at the same time maintain a crime-promoting penal system. They will not destroy the productive power of a nation and still expect it to be peaceful, prosperous, and democratic. They will not expect a world organization to be conjured into existence by semantically deranged "statesmen," before the necessary preceding integration of the constituent units has been achieved.

The development of the social sciences and the diffusion of scientific knowledge will doubtless greatly influence in the above ways the wants, wishes, and choices of men. But there is still an important difference between a statement of fact and the dictation of conduct. It is one thing for a physician to tell a patient: "Unless you undergo this operation, which will cost so much in time, money, and pain, you will probably die in one month." It is another matter to say: "Science, for which I am an accredited spokesman, says you shall undergo this operation." Any scientist who pretends that science authorizes him to make the latter statement is a fraud and a menace. Dictation of this type has not accompanied the rise of physical science and it need not result from the full maturity of the social sciences. This needs to be kept in mind especially in these days of much worry about brain trusts and whether, with the development of atomic fission, scientists must become a priestly class dictating all public policy.

The misunderstanding regarding the relation of scientists to practical affairs is so widespread and mischievous as to warrant further emphasis. The *application* of scientific knowledge obviously involves value judgments of some sort. This problem is equally present in the other sciences. After we know how to produce dynamite and what it will do, there remains the question: Shall we drop it from airplanes to destroy cathedrals and cities, or shall we use it to build roads through the montains? After we know the effects of certain drugs and gases, the question still remains: Shall we use them to alleviate pain and prevent disease, or shall we use them to destroy helpless and harmless populations? There is certainly nothing in the well-developed sciences of chemistry or physics which answers these questions. Neither is it the business of the social sciences to answer (except *conditionally,* as we have seen) the question of what form of government we should have, what our treatment of other races should be, whether we should tolerate or persecute certain religious groups, whether and to what degree civil liberties should be maintained, and a multitude of other questions which agitate us. What, then, are social scientists for and what should they be able to do?

Broadly speaking, it is the business of social scientists to be able to predict with high probability the social weather, just as meteorologists predict sunshine and storm. More specifically, social scientists should be able to say what is likely to happen socially under stated conditions. A competent economist or political scientist should be able to devise, for example, a tax program for a given country which will yield with high probability a certain revenue and which will fall in whatever desired degrees upon each of the income groups of the area concerned. Social scientists should be able to state also what will be the effect of the application of this program upon income, investments, consumption, production, and the outcome of the next election. Having devised such a tax program and clearly specified what it will do, it is not the business of the social scientists any more than it is the business of any other citizens to secure the adoption or defeat of such a program. In the same way, competent sociologists, educators, or psychologists should be able to advise a parent as to the most convenient way of converting a son into an Al Capone or into an approved citizen, according to what is desired.

My point is that no science tells us *what to do* with the knowledge that constitutes the science. Science only provides a car and a chauffeur for us. It does not directly, as science, tell us where to drive. The car and the chauffeur will take us into the ditch, over the precipice, against a stone wall, or into the highlands of age-long human aspirations with equal efficiency. If we agree as to where we want to go and tell the driver our goal, he should be able to take us there by any one of a number of possible routes, the costs and conditions of each of which the scientist should be able to explain to us. When these alternatives have been made clear, it is also a proper function of the scientist to devise the quickest and most reliable instrument for detecting the wishes of his passengers. But, except in his capacity as one of the passengers, the scientist who serves as navigator and chauffeur has no scientific privilege or duty to tell the rest of the passengers what they *should* want. There is nothing in either physical or social science which answers this question. Confusion on this point is, I think, the main reason for the common delusion that the social sciences, at least, must make value judgments of this kind.

But it does follow, as we have seen, that science, by virtue of its true function, as outlined above, may be of the utmost importance in helping people to decide intelligently what they want. The broad, general wants of people are perhaps everywhere highly uniform. They want, for example, a certain amount of physical and social security and some fun. It is disagreement over the means toward these ends, as represented by fantastic ideologies, that results in conflict and chaos. I have pointed out that, in proportion as a science is well developed, it can describe with accuracy *the consequences* of a variety of widely disparate programs of action. These consequences, if reliably predicted, are bound strongly to influence what people will want. But it remains a fact that science, in the sense of a predictor of consequences, is only *one* of the numerous influences that determine an individual's wants and his consequent behavior. Science and scientists are still the servants, not the masters, of mankind. Accordingly, those scientists who contend that they can scientifically determine not only the means but the ends of social policy should be exposed as scientific fakers as well as would-be dictators. Yet this is the very group which professes to be concerned about the undemocratic implications of the position I am here defending!

Finally, this view seems to some people to do away with what they call "the moral basis of society." Obviously, it does nothing of the sort. The question is not about the moral basis of society but about the social basis of morals. We merely advocate a scientific basis for morality. Presumably, all will agree that morals exist for man, not man for morals. Morals are those rules of conduct which man thinks have been to his advantage through the ages. Why should we then not all agree that we want the most authentic possible appraisal of that subject?

There appears, then, to be no reason why the methods of science cannot solve social problems. Neither should we expect more from social than from physical science. As *science,* both physical and social sciences have a common function, namely, to answer scientific questions. These answers will always be of an impersonal, conditional type: *"If* the temperature falls to 32°F., *then* water (H_2O) will freeze." "*If* a certain type of tax is adopted, *then* certain types of industrial activity will decrease." Neither of these statements carries any implications as to whether or how the knowledge should be used. Far from being a weakness, this characteristic of scientific knowledge is its greatest strength. The wants of men will change with changing conditions through the ages. The value of scientific knowledge lies precisely in this impersonal, neutral, general validity for whatever purposes man desires to use it.

For this reason, those scientists and others who try to identify science with some particular social program, sect, or party must be regarded as the most dangerous enemies of science. They are more dangerous than its avowed enemies, because the defenders of "democratic," "communist," "religious," or "moral" science pose as defenders of science and carry on their agitation in the name of lofty social sentiments. That this group is confused rather than malicious is evident from their proposal that scientists should take an oath not to engage in scientific activity which may be "destructive" or contrary to "toleration," "justice," etc. The absurdity of the proposal is readily apparent, if we consider any actual scientific work. No scientist can foresee all the uses to which his work may be put, and in any event it is a commonplace that the *same* drug may be used to cure or to kill people. It may be granted that preposterous proposals of this kind are a temporary hysterical phenomenon superinduced by such dramatic developments as the atomic bomb. It may be granted that the agitators are motivated by lofty social sentiments. Unfortunately, the same has been said for prominent proponents of the Inquisition.[29]

The uses to which scientific or other knowledge is to be put have always been and will continue to be a legitimate concern of men. Science, as we have noted, can be valuable in helping men to decide that question. Our warning here has been directed against attempts to corrupt scientific methods and results by allowing them to be influenced by the temporary, provincial, ethnocentric preferences of particular scientists or pressure groups.*

D. Conclusion

WE HAVE ENUMERATED above the major postulates of science and their corollaries which have special significance for sociology. Many of these points will be further elaborated in the next two chapters.

Our principal concern in the present chapter has been to emphasize that the apparent difference between the data of the "physical" and the social sciences springs chiefly from a failure to recognize that the immediate data of *all* sciences are human responses to whatever arouses those responses. Much of scientific development depends, as we shall see, upon the type of symbols we develop to represent the phenomena to which we respond. We need only suggest in this connection what would be the state of any of our sciences if arabic numerals, the zero, and the calculus had never been invented. With these symbols and the rules governing their use, any fourth-grade child can solve problems—relevant, important problems—which staggered the most brilliant intellect of ancient Greece. Clearly it makes a difference with what symbolic equipment we approach our scientific tasks. It would be strange indeed if this lesson from the other sciences should be entirely inapplicable to the study of sociological problems.

This point has been emphasized not so much to minimize the uniqueness and intricacy of societal phenomena as to suggest the type of approach to which these difficulties are most likely to yield. It is not necessary to argue that societal and "physical" data are the "same," or "similar." No phenomena in the universe are identical and to admit that societal phenomena are "different" from "physical" is a highly irrelevant concession in the present context unless we fur-

* That such a warning is in order appears from a recent study by S. S. West. Only one-third of the fifty-seven researchers in six science departments of a major midwestern university took the view that the scientist, as scientist, is completely neutral in his concern for how the knowledge is applied. About one-fourth felt they could separate their roles as scientists and citizens, remaining neutral in the one but stating their position in the other. (Reported in "Scientists vs. the Ideology of Science," *The American Behavioral Scientist,* Vol. 4, March, 1961, p. 35.)

ther specify *in what respect* we allege they are different. *All* phenomena are different in some respects. *All* of them are similar in one highly vital respect, namely, in that they are all known, if at all, through sense experience conceptualized and organized into the patterns determined by the nature of the human organism as conditioned by all its environments. This is the only similarity relevant to the present discussion because we are concerned at present only with the means by which valid knowledge of *any* phenomena is achieved. Are the means by which we know societal phenomena fundamentally different from the means by which we know physical phenomena? If they are not, then it is as irrelevant for our present purpose to enumerate "differences" between "physical" and societal phenomena as it would be to claim that the differences between ants, spiders, and grasshoppers preclude a science of biology. Indeed, all discussion of similarities and differences of phenomena without specifying explicitly or through the context with respect to what aspect of the phenomena we are concerned may be said to be quite meaningless. Such discussion is not uncommon in sociological treatises on differences between societal and "physical" phenomena.

Much has been said in this connection about the ability of "physical" scientists to bring their "subject-matters" (i.e., the referents of their symbolized responses) into the laboratory and otherwise manipulate them. This possibility varies considerably with different sciences. The solar system has never been brought into any laboratory. Astronomical laboratories do contain very ingenious symbolic and mechanical representations of the astronomical aspects of that system and remarkable instruments for observing it. These every science must unquestionably develop. Beyond this, the question of laboratory conditions becomes one of convenience and technical and mechanical ingenuity. Already it is possible to observe illuminating sociological situations in the laboratory through sound and motion pictures, not to mention the extensive sociological experiments involving laboratory observations of children and college students.

In short, most of us have been brought up in a world in which we are taught that the physical sciences deal with metals, fluids, gases, and such "matter" which we like to describe with such reassuring sounds as "tangible," "visible," "actual," "real." The phenomena of the social sciences, on the other hand, we have been taught to consider "intangible," and "invisible" entities described by words like customs, mores, competition, sovereignty, justice, etc. Yet these words if they mean anything at all, certainly refer to *behavior—events* impinging on our senses. The aspects of the universe with which chemists and physicists deal, and which folk-language designates by such broad categories as metals, fluids, and gases refer just as certainly to *other* behavior events. Yet such is the tendency for us to project upon nature the structure of our language that we develop a superstitious reverence for the categories that are merely constructs which man somewhere, sometime, found a convenient framework within which to assort his experiences.[30]

To those who still find that these traditional frameworks serve their purposes, the present essay has nothing to offer. There are doubtless also those who still find the pre-Copernican astronomy, pre-Newtonian physics, and pre-Darwinian biology quite adequate to their needs. But they will perhaps find themselves increasingly disturbed by the intrusions and by-products of the scientific quest as represented by our technological age. Frequently the findings of that quest will, as Veblen said, "go beyond the breaking-point of their jungle-fed spiritual sensibilities." At such times they will "furtively or by an overt breach of consistency . . . seek comfort in marvelous articles of savage-born lore." [31] Take, for example, the following honest confession of a distinguished president of Columbia University in 1873. President Barnard had himself specialized in the natural sciences, served as president of the American Association for the Advancement of Science, and was noted for his liberal views. With reference to the doctrine of evolution he said:

"Much as I love truth in the abstract I love my sense of immortality still more; and if the final outcome of all the boasted discoveries of modern science is to disclose to men that they are more evanescent than the shadow of the swallow's wing upon the lake . . . if this, after all is the best that science can give me, give me then, I pray, no more science. I will live on in my simple ignorance, as my fathers did before me; and when I shall at length be sent to my final repose, let me . . . lie down to pleasant, even though they may be deceitful dreams." [32]

To those who find themselves in this unhappy predicament I can only say with Bentley: [33]

"I can deeply sympathize with anyone who objects to being tossed into such a floating cosmology. Much as I have stressed its substantiality, I can hardly expect everyone to feel it. The firm land of 'matter' or even of 'sense' or 'self' is pleasanter, if only it stands firm. To anyone whose tasks can be performed on such ground, I have not the slightest thought of bringing disturbance. But for many of us tasks are pressing, in the course of which our firmest spots of conventional departure themselves dissolve in function. When they have so dissolved, and when we are so involved, there is no hope of finding refuge in some chance island of 'fact' which may appear. The continents go, and the islands. The pang may be like that felt by a confirmed landsman at his first venture on the ocean, but the ocean in time becomes familiar and secure. Or, if I may change the figure, the fledgling will vastly prefer his firm nest to falling with untried wings. But the parent sciences are pushing; the nest, even, is disintegrating; and there is air for flight, even though it is not so vividly felt and seen as the sticks and straws of the nest."

E. Notes

1. It is still conventional in sociology to refer to adjustment in terms of an organism's "striving" or "need" for "certain ends." For many purposes this anthropomorphic terminology is useful. But for the sake of consistency with the terminology of other sciences, we propose to deal with the phenomena in question in a framework in which the terms "needs" and "ends" are unnecessary. It is possible to interpret the event of a stone rolling down a hill into a brook as a striving or a need of the stone for the brook, and in many other terms and frameworks of which ethnology furnishes various examples. But in the scientific frame of reference we have adopted and defined operationally such terms as "mass," "gravity," and "field of force," as more suitable for our purpose. That purpose in science is to explain as much as possible by as few terms or symbols as possible—the principle of parsimony. We adopt here the viewpoint of modern psychology that the behavior of nervous tissue and of organisms is explicable in the same basic terms as the behavior of other matter. In this orientation, "needs" become merely biophysical or biochemical imbalances in an organism or between it and its environment. Cf. John Dewey, *Logic. The Theory of Inquiry,* Holt, 1939, p. 27: "The state of disturbed equilibration constitutes *need.*" That organisms behave with reference to the anticipated results of the behavior is, of course, admitted,

as is all other observed behavior. In our frame of reference such "ends" whenever they figure in a behavior situation exist in the form of symbols of some kind and organisms respond to these symbols just as they respond to other stimuli. These symbols and whatever they stand for are from our point of view merely part of the data of the situation, and have the same power of influencing conduct as any other phenomena that precipitate responses. The present treatment assumes an elementary knowledge of modern psychology and physiology.

The above position should dispel the curious notion that behavioristic or positivistic theory denies or ignores the problems of ends, values, etc., in behavior. For example R. K. Merton ("Durkheim's Division of Labor in Society," *Amer. Journ. of Sociology*, XL, Nov., 1934, p. 321) says: "For, if, as positivism would have us believe, logic and science can deal only with empirical facts, with sensa, then a science of social phenomena, on that score alone becomes impossible, since this attitude relegates to the limbo all ends [*sic*] i.e., subjective anticipations of *future* occurrences without a consideration of which human behavior becomes inexplicable." The symbols by and through which man anticipates the future or in terms of which he reacts to any "ends" are as tangible and objective phenomena as any other that precipitate behavior. If any positivist or behaviorist actually held such views as those attributed to them above, there would, of course, be ample ground for agitation on the part of the critics. But even J. B. Watson, whose more popular works are usually relied upon to furnish unguarded statements susceptible of such interpretation, was quite explicit and emphatic on the above point. "Let me make this fundamental point at once: that *saying* is doing—that is *behaving*. Speaking overtly or to ourselves (thinking) is just as objective a type of behavior as baseball." (*Behaviorism*, Norton, 1924, p. 6.) See also my paper "Is Sociology Too Scientific?" *Sociologus*, IX, Sept., 1933, pp. 311-312. Also C. L. Hull "Goal Attraction and Directing Ideas Conceived as Habit Phenomena," *Psychological Review*, XXXVIII, 1931 (pp. 487-506). Also note 19 below.

2. It may be well to indicate briefly at this point my general position regarding the allegedly "mental" character of societal phenomena. For illustrative purposes I refer to some statements in the otherwise unobjectionable discussion by L. von Wiese and H. Becker, *Systematic Sociology*, Wiley, 1932, Ch. II, p. 33. E.g., "To be sure, our senses can perceive only *concrete objects,* in the form of discrete human bodies, and between them only the atmosphere, other organisms, and inorganic matter. *Plurality patterns themselves cannot be thus perceived* and can be made corporeally apparent only by symbols. Nevertheless, many of them are recognizable in our *internal world* of presentations, concepts and images. They live in the minds of tangible human beings, men, in the neuro-psychic patterns

of human beings." [Italics mine.] (See also the section heading of the same page which reads: "Plurality patterns are not perceivable, but nevertheless are real." If we investigate wherein resides the "concreteness" of the "objects" which our senses perceive, we would probably be forced to agree with Bentley (*Behavior Knowledge Fact,* Principia Press, pp. 209-210), who in a brilliant chapter on "The Visibility of the Social," remarks: "Not that the words 'concrete' and 'abstract' have significance in modern scientific application; they are nebulous wraiths surviving from primitive man's attempts at description, serving today merely for the crudest contrasts and reports." When our senses perceive "concrete objects" we respond to behavior of some sort (i.e., light rays from an object strike the optic nerve). If this reaction ever becomes knowledge to us at all, i.e., if we symbolize it, we do so because the response (usually symbolized) fits into a system of past responses (also usually symbolized) as a frame of reference which gives the response meaning. If we say that certain social structures exist it is likewise because our senses react to some behavior. We symbolize this response into "presentations," "images," and "concepts." Then *these* (in common with our images of "concrete" objects) "live" in our "minds" and the minds of those to whom we may be able to communicate. In short, Wiese and Becker overlook in the above case the "concrete objects" (behavior) from which they derive their symbolic "image" of social structures, and in the other case overlook the *symbolic process* by which they derive the "images" of the "concrete objects"—in both cases because traditional philosophy and logic (symbolic systems) have thoroughly habituated us to (in fact require) such dichotomies between the "social" (human) and the "physical." The dichotomy is in the nature of a primary postulate taken over perhaps from theology. There is no support whatever for the postulate in modern science. Wiese and Becker come very near to my position later in the same section when they say: "Strictly speaking, a social structure never consists of human beings but of images, presentations and concepts which may be traced back to relationships. . . . *Relationship-structures exist only in and through human ideas.*" [Italics mine.] If they would say the same for *all* knowledge we would be agreed. I would say that our knowledge of "social" *and* "physical" structure-relationships consists of images, etc., which may be traced back to *that which* evoked them.

I am in full accord with the following estimate of Wiese's position by Bentley ("Sociology and Mathematics," *Sociological Review,* XXIII, 1931): "Turning to recent German sociology, the development of L. von Wiese is the one most fully in accord with what is here attempted. Taking his initiative from Simmel's presentation of forms of socialization as do all of the more important recent German sociologists, Wiese stresses as fundamental the immediate and direct observation of a realm of social fact. This is his 'sozial Optik' vital to his entire work. Differing from the present approach, however, he coordinates the social realm with the physical and psychical realms: accepting these latter as he finds them in their respective lines of scientific investigation: and demanding only for the social its full right to its own independent investigation, on a par with the others. In this social realm he finds possibilities of measuring and counting: and these are not mere borrowings from other sciences, but are peculiarly social techniques." (P. 160.) Because of this he asserts the existence of a peculiarly social space, "without, however, proceeding to a fully functional analysis of it in system with physical space presentations." The physical space therefore appears as an outlying or indirect "cause" of happenings in social space, and not as an intimately involved region of the full sociological investigation. (P. 161.)

Significant in this connection is Wiese's attempt to derive "sociologically usable materials through intensive analysis of words denoting relations, etc." He reports (Wiese-Becker, *Systematic Sociology,* p. 129) that a seminar at the University of Cologne devoted itself to lexicographic research over a period of years with the object of listing all words with "definite sociological meaning." "It soon became evident," he says, "that the plan covered too much territory, for in spite of relatively minute divisions of labor a full year was consumed in working through the letter A." While lists of such words may be of historical interest and while they may be suggestive of behavior phenomena to be looked for, the words thus found are unfortunately too frequently accorded quite other significance. It is assumed that since the word exists, it must have a counterpart in nature, and any system which leaves out the *word* is therefore defective. To include all words *as data* in sociology is obviously entirely different from including all the vague allusions of folklore-words in the vocabulary of scientific sociology. It is the latter tendency which is here under criticism.

In this connection I am also in agreement with the following criticism of a position which has been put forward by K. Lewin (*Principles of Topological Psychology,* McGraw-Hill, 1936) and J. F. Brown (*Psychology and the Social Order,* McGraw-Hill, 1936): "Although efforts have recently been made to distinguish two types of empirical statement, 'the language of data' and the 'language of constructs,' it appears evident to the psychologist that the dichotomy is artificial. A statement about a datum is a statement about a construct. The simple statement, 'I see red,' is a complex response conditional upon previous training and present circumstances of an organism and differs only in complexity from a statement such as, 'The oscillograph shows that the discharge takes place at a potential of 80 volts.' The notion of a language of Data is reminiscent of the concept of an absolute 'given' and since it can be shown that the immediately given experience is defined operationally as consisting of relatively elementary differential responses, we had best dispense with the distinction between data and constructs." (Pp. 99-100, S. S. Stevens "Psychology: The Propaedeutic Science," *Philosophy of Science,* IV, Jan., 1936, pp. 90-103.) See also note 6 below.

3. Cf. P. W. Bridgman, *The Logic of Modern Physics,* Macmillan, 1932, p. 37. Failure to recognize this point has been the basis of much futile controversy such for example as the contention that statistics may *describe* but can never *explain* a situation. This position usually assumes that true "explanation" must always be in terms of lower levels, e.g., psychology in terms of physiology, physiology in terms of chemistry, etc., J. F. Brown (*op. cit.*), and K. Lewin (*A Dynamic Theory of Personality,* McGraw-Hill, 1935), also seem to repudiate on other but equally fallacious grounds, the value of classification as a predictive devise. If it has been established statistically that children lose their teeth at a certain age, then the classification of a child as of that age explains, in the sense defined above, the loss of his teeth and enables us to predict the event. Curiosity about the biological sequences leading up to that event is *also* desirable and the satisfaction of such curiosity (i.e., reducing the phenomenon to elements with which we are so familiar that we accept them as a matter of course) is a type of explanation on another level. Such explanation consists of classifying this particular phenomenon under some general and already established generalization of biology. That generalization is in the last analysis based on precisely the same kind of repeated observation as is the generalization that children of certain age group lose their teeth. Such reduction is, of course, desirable in the pursuit of relatively comprehensive and unified knowledge and the suggestion by Brown and Lewin that we need *further* explanation of social phenomena in terms of the field structure within which they operate is quite true. It is an overstatement, however, to claim that classification is without explanatory or predictive value.

4. I use the word "physical" in quotation marks in order to emphasize that I do not recognize this word as denoting, for scientific purposes, any unique character of the phenomena to which this word is usually used to refer as contrasted with the phenomena designated "social," "cultural," etc. Since all phenomena are "physical" from my point of view, I retain the word only to designate a conventional distinction which must be defined, if at all, only in terms of the degree of universality and uniformity of responses of human beings to some phenomena as contrasted with others.

5. "Through the frosted windows of our senses we may say, if we please, that we receive impressions of what we call the 'external universe' or 'reality.' But it is not necessary to say anything so mystical—at least

for the present. It is sufficient to recall that certain scientific philosophers are content to start from the sense impressions themselves as 'reality' without seeking for anything less familiar and more disputable. Einstein for one, in his paper of 1936, appears to be satisfied to identify reality provisionally with the sense impressions which others refer to a yet more recondite reality." (E. T. Bell, *The Handmaiden of the Sciences,* Williams & Wilkins, 1937, pp. 17, 18. See also note 13 below.)

6. This statement should not be understood to mean that I consider sensory experience as an absolute datum or starting point in the sense that Hume and Hobbes (to mention no others before and since) seem to have held. I take rather the position of E. C. Singer (*Mind as Behavior,* R. G. Adams and Co., Columbus, 1924) which regards the immediate datum as an *ideal terminus* of abstraction. What we have to work with as immediate data are our *knowledge* of sensory experience, i.e., inferences (symbolic representations), from sensation. "The purely objective world and the purely subjective datum of consciousness are two ideals toward which we can endlessly strive, modifying our notions of each as we change our understanding of the other. . . . It is only in this process of reconstruction that the concepts of 'consciousness' and 'object of consciousness' fall out —*they fall out together,* and together they grow apace. To follow the adventures of this pair is, I suspect, to be led deep into the heart of things." (P. 30) For elaboration of the point see Singer, *op. cit.,* Ch. 9 on "Sensation and the Datum of Science." See also William James, *Principles of Psychology,* I, p. 508. See also John Dewey, *op. cit.,* p. 38: "In a proper conception of experience, inference, reasoning and conceptual structures are as experiential as is observation, and . . . the fixed separation between the former and the latter has no warrant beyond an episode in the history of culture." Also W. V. Metcalf, "The Reality of the Atom," *Philosophy of Science,* VI, July, 1939, pp. 368, 370: "And just what is this fundamental philosophical distinction between 'percept' and 'concept'? —the 'percept' of the 'real' table and of the 'real' meteor, and the 'concept' of the atom? . . . Are they not both mental constructs of what we have come to believe exists in the external world? . . . The view that seems to me worth emphasizing is that *all* our beliefs in external reality are the result of inference from our subjective sense-data."

7. Under this definition, objectivity is always a matter of degree and is always relative to the sensory equipment and general response capacities of responding organisms. The phenomena corroborated by everyone are thus considered the most objective. Corroboration by all or most "qualified observers" is frequently substituted for mere preponderance of general opinion in cases where the prestige of the "qualified" is such that we accept their responses as more valid than our own. This viewpoint is further elaborated later in this chapter. (See points 3 and 4.) Cf. Aris-

totle: "Whatever appears true to everybody must be accepted as such; and he who denies the validity of universal opinion can hardly produce any more valid criterion of his own." (*Aristotle, from Natural Science, Psychology, and The Nicomachean Ethics,* Translated by P. H. Wheelwright, Doubleday, 1935, p. 212.)

8. James Harvey Robinson in *The Story of Human Error,* Appleton-Century, 1936, p. 276, edited by Joseph Jastrow. The quotation is attributed to Professor Woodworth.

9. E.g., Morris Cohen's categorical statement "Psychic forces are not physical forces." *Reason and Nature,* Harcourt, 1931, p. 360.

10. R. M. MacIver, *op. cit.,* pp. 476-477. [Italics mine.]

11. See A. Einstein and L. Infeld, *The Evolution of Physics,* Simon and Schuster, 1938, p. 33.

12. *Ibid.* It is interesting to note that this, on the whole, excellent statement runs afoul of itself on account of the speech habits which even these authors are unable to avoid when they attempt popular exposition. Note the contradiction in the sentence in italics in the text. My criticism in the text is directed at precisely this lingustic habit of talking about "*real mechanisms*" of which we "cannot *even imagine* the possibility or meaning" as compared to our conception of them!

13. *Ibid.,* pp. 158, 159. Cf. also the following passages from these authors:

"The [electromagnetic] field *did not exist* for the physicist of the early years of the Nineteenth Century." (P. 157.)

"There would be no place in our new physics, for both field and matter, *field being the only reality,*" ... "But we have not yet succeeded in formulating a pure field physics. For the present we must still assume the existence of both: field and matter." (Pp. 258, 260.) [Italics mine.]

"The reality created by modern physics is, indeed, far removed from the reality of the early days. But the aim of every physical theory still remains the same.... Quantum physics formulates laws governing crowds and not individuals. Not properties but probabilities are described, not laws disclosing the future of systems are formulated, but laws governing the changes in time of the probabilities and relating to great congregations of individuals." (Pp. 312-313.)

"But what I am trying to do is to push the analysis so far back that we are asking ourselves what it means to say that a world really 'exists' independently of ourselves and our sensations. I am trying to point out that any meaning I find in making such a statement is found in things *which I do* and experience, of which I am aware." (P. W. Bridgman, *The Intelligent Individual and Society,* Macmillan, 1938, pp. 152-153.) [Italics mine.]

The following statement by A. P. Weiss has, I think, never been improved upon:

"Metaphysics, for the behaviorist, is merely a name for special types of linguistic habits that have been acquired by reading other books on metaphysics, rhetoric, grammar, etc. A metaphysical analysis is essentially an analysis of a verbal statement of some sort into other verbal statements that are historically related. . . . One of the problems of science is that of determining the antecedent conditions which precede the appearance of some experimental or technical result. Next the antecedents of the antecedents are isolated, and so the investigations are continued backward until a stage is reached beyond which experimental analysis or observation has not gone. The usefulness of any guess as to the nature of unobserved antecedents depends upon how well the guess is verified when the experimental technique will have been refined to the point at which a testing of the validity of the guess or prediction is possible. Thus, until recently by following this method, the chemist regarded the atom, of which he postulated aout ninety different kinds, as the ultimate unit or element in the structure of matter. As experimentation became more refined, the guess of ninety different kinds of elements was not verified. A new guess was proposed by the physicists,—the electron-proton hypothesis, in which the number of units was reduced to two. For the physicist, then, the electron-proton hypothesis is a guess as to what would be observed visually with a microscope of sufficient magnifying power. On the whole it is to be expected that the physicist who *uses* the microscope, *performs* the laboratory analysis and then *reports* the results, should be better qualified to guess the nature of the antecedents of what he observes than the professional metaphysician who has available only the verbal report of the physicist.

"The metaphysical problem as it presents itself for analysis, can only be a study of the biosocial antecedents of the language responses (metaphysical discussions) recorded in the literature as the verbo-motor responses of individuals who, for the time being, are classified as metaphysicians. The *scientific* solution is thus narrowed down to an investigation of the metaphysician's heredity and training. All metaphysical discussions, no matter how profound and involved they may be, are in the *last* analysis nothing but language responses and linguistic habits derived from other language responses. In science, observation and the analysis of experiential conditions play a much larger part. When the metaphysical problem is stated in the form of the question, What are the essentials of reality? the term *reality* for the behaviorist is merely a word stimulus which individuals of a given social status use to designate the fact that the responses occurring at any one moment might be more complex and varied than they actually are if the bodily response mechanism were more complex than it really is.

"Thus I may affirm that the clock in my room has an existence or reality aside from my reactions to it because of the following behavior conditions. Suppose one of my responses is that of counting the ticks. The number of ticks that can be counted seems to be unlimited, but the manner of counting may be continuous or intermittent. The alternative responses of counting or not counting are not determined by the nature of the clock. That is, if I had installed an automatic counter for the ticks, the visual readings of this counter would be correlative with *continuous* auditory counting, but not with *intermittent* auditory counting. In terms of behavior this only means that some responses (oral counting) and other responses (visual counting) are sometimes correlated, sometimes not, and that the cause of this correlation is some condition (clock) that is independent of my own body.

"Reality is merely the term that designates this type of relationship between responses. It is the basis of the fiction of an external world of stimuli. This particular fiction, as a form of behavior, has persisted. Another fiction, characterized as solipsism, has never been generally adopted. According to this fiction my own responses are the only responses that ever occur. Certainly I have never found myself doing anything else. When I am not reacting (as in dreamless sleep) there is only oblivion. For the behaviorist, then, the problem of the nature of reality is a biosocial problem of tracing out the type of behavior which corresponds to the assumption that there is an external reality of which man is only a part and that this assumption has survived longer (produced better cooperation between individuals) than any other." (A. P. Weiss, *A Theoretical Basis of Human Behavior*, R. G. Adams, 1929, pp. 44-47.)

14. E.g., R. M. MacIver, *Society: Its Structure and Changes*, Long and Smith, 1931, p. 45. "They seek to apply mechanical methods of measurement to *things whose very nature they fail to understand*." [Italics mine.]

15. Ellsworth Faris, "The Primary Group: Essence and Accident," *Amer. Journ. of Soc.*, XXXVIII, July, 1932, p. 44.

16. *Ibid.*, p. 45.

17. *Ibid.*

18. See J. B. Watson, *op. cit.* (See note 1 above.)

19. The relatively undeveloped state of the methods of study of symbolic behavior has, of course, given rise to the usual conclusion that these phenomena are, as T. Parsons has said, "outside the range of scientific observation and analysis." (*The Structure of Social Action*, McGraw-Hill, 1937, p. 421.) In this work, the author says: "It will be maintained and the attempt made in considerable detail to prove that *in this sense* [as a general framework for understanding human behavior] *all of the versions of*

positivistic social thought constitute untenable positions, for both empirical and methodological reasons." [P. 125. Italics in the original.] In so far as a single statement may be selected as illustrative of the type of consideration which the author has in mind, the following is suggestive with respect to the matter here under discussion: "If a stone is at the same time a religious symbol, there is a double symbolic reference when the word 'stone,' or a particular of that class, is spoken or thought: first, a reference of the word to the object; second, that of the object, in turn, to that which it symbolizes. In the case of an imaginary entity, the situation is *in essentials* the same, except that the immediate reference of the original linguistic symbol is not mediated through sense data *in the same way.* Zeus is not experienced *in the same sense* as a stone." [P. 423. Italics mine.] I assume that the author means by imaginary entities precisely the type of "imaginings" and "echoes" I have discussed in the main text and, if so, that discussion also applies to this illustration. To me, the significant admission is that the imaginary situation is *"in essentials* the same," for I consider the essential similarity in this context to be the observability and the possibility of objectively designating the phenomenon. If so, it is, as I have noted in the main text, entirely unnecessary that there should be any other "sameness" in the situations. In short, echoes and shadows may be "mediated" in a vast variety of ways, but we do not therefore contend that they are not experienced "in the same sense."

20. M. A. Copeland, "Desire, Choice and Purpose from a Natural-Evolutionary Viewpoint," *Psychological Review,* XXXIII, p. 145, 1926.

21. See R. K. Merton, *op. cit.,* p. 321. See note 1 above.

22. See J. F. Markey, *The Symbolic Process and Its Integration in Children,* Harcourt, 1928, pp. 141, 142, 146, 147. Also John Dewey *Experience and Nature,* Norton, 1925, pp. 322 ff. G. H. Mead, "The Genesis of Self and Social Control," *International Journal of Ethics,* XXXV, 1924-25, pp. 251-277.

23. See W. Köhler, *Gestalt Psychology,* Liveright, 1929. Also K. Koffka, *Principles of Gestalt Psychology,* Harcourt, 1935.

I am unable to see that there is anything in the approach of these and other authors of the so-called "Gestalt school" which justifies its designation as a unique "school." Their experimental work is frequently excellent, but I find no difficulty in interpreting their findings in the behavioristic terms of A. P. Weiss or other competent behavioristic writers. Much of the "Gestalt" attack seems to me to be directed at a bogey usually called the "atomistic-mechanistic" approach, the alleged sponsors of which are usually not cited, and I have been unable to find anyone who supports the position referred to. In so far as the Gestalt position can be identified with the field theory as advanced by J. F. Brown (*Psychology and the Social Order*), I find myself largely in agreement with it. But the whole-part relationship to which Gestalt psychology is supposed to have made special contributions does not seem to me to have been at all clarified by the turgid treatment of Gestalt writers. Fine literary phrases such as "the whole is more than the sum of its parts," derive their impressiveness chiefly from their obscurity. The problem when objectively examined is quite simple. Consider the much quoted illustration of hydrogen and oxygen considered separately and in the compound H_2O. Is the latter "more than the sum of" the former? The question has no sensible operational meaning. All that needs to be pointed out is that hydrogen and oxygen act upon *different sense organs* (or act differently upon the same sense organs) when combined into H_2O than when uncombined. That they should give us a *different* sensation in combination than in separation is, therefore, no mystery requiring weird philosophical conjuring about the whole-part relationship. One is neither more nor less than the other. They produce different sensations, each of which is equally "real," "whole," and otherwise a legitimate phenomenon for study. This is perhaps generally recognized with respect to such phenomena as are used in the above illustration. But when the same problem rises as between "man" and "society" it sometimes gives rise to protracted futile discussion.

24. J. A. Thomson and P. Geddes, *Life: Outlines of General Biology,* Harper, 1932, II, p. 1413.

25. See L. L. Bernard "The Evolution of Social Consciousness and of the Social Sciences," *Psy. Rev.,* XXXIX, March, 1932, pp. 147-164, for a discussion of the reasons for the earlier development of some sciences.

26. E. T. Bell, *op. cit.,* pp. 104, 105.

27. C. P. Snow, "The Moral Un-Neutrality of Science," Address to the 127th Meeting of the A.A.A.S., New York, 1960, printed in *Science,* January 27, 1961, pp. 255-261.

28. *Hearings Before a Subcommittee of the Committee on Military Affairs,* U.S. Senate, 79th Congress, First Session, Parts I-V, *Congressional Record,* p. 8164. See also G. A. Lundberg, "The Senate Ponders Social Science," *Scientific Monthly,* 1947, pp. 397-411.

29. For further elaboration of this whole subject, see G. Lundberg, "Science, Scientists, and Values," *Social Forces,* May, 1952, pp. 373-379.

30. It is unfortunately not possible here to give an adequate account of the full extent to which linguistic and semantic difficulties at present handicap the social sciences. The reader is urged to supplement the present chapter by readings from the following sources. The first two sources are popular and elementary treatises. Stuart Chase, *The Tyranny of Words,* Harcourt, 1938. Thurman W. Arnold, *The Folklore of Capitalism,* Yale University Press, 1937. P. W. Bridgman, *The Logic of Modern Physics,* Macmillan, 1932. C. K. Ogden and I. A. Richards, *The Meaning*

of Meaning, Rev. Ed., Harcourt, 1936. Alfred Korzybski, *Science and Sanity,* Science Press, 1933. J. F. Markey, *The Symbolic Process and Its Integration in Children,* Harcourt, 1928. By far the best brief source is C. W. Morris, "Foundations of the Theory of Signs," *International Encyclopedia of Unified Science,* I, Univ. of Chicago Press, 1938. Consider, for example, the following extracts:

"No contradiction arises in saying that every sign has a designatum but not every sign refers to an actual existent. Where what is referred to actually exists as referred to, the object of reference is a *denotatum.* It thus becomes clear that, while every sign has a designatum, not every sign has a denotatum. A designatum is not a thing, but a kind of object or class of objects—and a class may have many members, or one member, or no members. The denotata are the members of the class. This distinction makes explicable the fact that one may reach in the icebox for an apple that is not there and make preparations for living on an island that may never have existed or has long since disappeared beneath the sea." (P. 5.)

By "actual existent" Morris here apparently means those stimuli-phenomena which evoke universal or at least very general confirmatory responses in all or large numbers of men. The explanation of the behavior of reaching for the apple which "is there" and the apple which "is not there" lies in the description of the sequence or combination of events leading up to the reaching. This set of events will be different in the two cases, but subject to description within the same framework. Morris continues:

"The interpreter of a sign is an organism; the interpretant is the habit of the organism to respond, because of the sign vehicle, to absent objects which are relevant to a present problematic situation as if they were present. In virtue of semiosis an organism takes account of relevant properties of absent objects, or unobserved properties of objects which are present, and in this lies the general instrumental significance of ideas. Given the sign vehicle as an object of response, the organism expects a situation of such and such a kind and, on the basis of this expectation, can partially prepare itself in advance for what may develop. The response to things through the intermediacy of signs is thus biologically a continuation of the same process in which the distance senses have taken precedence over the contact senses in the control of conduct in higher animal forms; such animals through sight, hearing, and smell are already responding to distant parts of the environment through certain properties of objects functioning as signs of other properties. This process of taking account of a constantly more remote environment is simply continued in the complex processes of semiosis made possible by language, the object taken account of no longer needing to be perceptually present. (Pp. 31-32.)

... "If, following the lead of the pragmatist, mental phenomena be equated with sign responses, consciousness with reference by signs, and rational (or "free") behavior with the control of conduct in terms of foreseen consequences made available by signs, then psychology and the social sciences may recognize what is distinctive in their tasks and at the same time see their place within a unified science. Indeed, it does not seem fantastic to believe that the concept of sign may prove as fundamental to the sciences of man as the concept of cell for the biological sciences." (P. 42.)

31. T. Veblen, *The Place of Science in Modern Civilization*, Viking, 1932, pp. 26, 27.

32. Quoted by Sidney Ratner, "Evolution and the Rise of the Scientific Spirit in America," *Phil. of Sci.*, III, Jan.,1936, p. 115. For a good summary of the present scientific status of "materialism" see William Seifriz, "A Materialistic Interpretation of Life," *Phil. of Sci.*, VI, July, 1939, pp. 266-284.

33. A. F. Bentley, *Behavior Knowledge Fact*, Principia Press, 1935, p. 183.

Chapter II

SYMBOLIC BEHAVIOR AND THE PROBLEM OF QUANTIFICATION[1]

A. The Role of Symbols and Symbolic Systems in Society and in Science

NOTHING IS SO LIKELY to give offense as an inquiry into the meaning of the eloquent phrases in which social scientists today for the most part attempt to communicate. The linguistic noises to which we have become emotionally conditioned seem a peculiarly personal and private possession upon which we rely to a great extent for the projection of our personalities. To submit a person's language to ruthless analysis is quite generally regarded as a personal attack through the medium of sympathetic magic or otherwise. "Hair splitting," "garbling," "distortion" are favorite epithets for those who meddle with other people's language. Still more general is the feeling that "fine" points in linguistic tools do not matter, and are merely a way by which "smart alecks" call attention to themselves. This may be the case, of course. Nevertheless, we shall here take the view that a careful scrutiny of the fitness of our linguistic tools is perhaps of greater importance than a loquacious use of them.

The vocabulary, grammar, and literary style of the more fluent and eloquent talkers and writers represent in a very real sense a vested interest. Words are, furthermore, frequently the smoke screen which protect more tangible interests. This is not to imply that the defenders of such vested interests recognize them as such any more than do the defenders of vested interests in other fields. We all tend to have a deep feeling of the essential fitness of the words to which we have become accustomed. There are unquestionably thousands who feel that "pigs are rightly so-called because they are such dirty animals." They are at one with the traveler who, after recounting the strange words which are used in various lands to describe H_2O, concluded: "Now in English, as you know, we call it water, which is, of course, *what it really is.*"

We are not here primarily concerned with the vast amount of misunderstanding among people in daily conversation on account of the inadequacy of their language as a means of communication. Neither shall we elaborate upon the ambiguities, obscurities, and nonsense which professors, preachers, statesmen, politicians, and journalists frequently regurgitate to their publics.[2] We are concerned here mainly with the same problem as it affects the social sciences. As an illustration of the type of impasse into which an inadequate symbolic system is likely to force us, we may refer to Zeno's well-known paradox of Achilles and the tortoise. If Achilles allowed the tortoise a head start in a race, it was suggested, the former could never overtake the latter. Whatever common sense and an actual trial might show, the language and the logic in terms of which the paradox was set up left no escape from the strange conclusion. The tortoise is allowed 100 yards start. Although Achilles runs ten times as fast as the tortoise, the latter will obviously have gone an additional ten yards by the time Achilles has run the first hundred yards. When Achilles has run this additional ten yards, the tortoise will still be one yard ahead. By this process of verbalization about the race it is obvious that while Achilles is constantly getting nearer to the tortoise he can never quite overtake it.

If instead of the above method of symbolizing this event we resort to a simple algebraic or geometric statement [3] of a type unknown to the Greeks, we come to very different conclusions. We find by the latter methods (under given assumptions) that Achilles definitely overtakes the tortoise at the end of 111.11 seconds. What is more important, this result also corresponds to what happens in an actual experiment. This verifiable result of the latter method suggests that perhaps it is preferable as a symbolic device for such mundane matters as, for example, planning the dispatch of trains. The former method may be more advantageous in "creating" thrilling situations in imaginative literature, which unquestionably has recreational value; but we are interested here in symbolic systems which will be reliable charts to adjustments beyond the universe of the symbols themselves.

When applied to simple and familiar events of everyday observation, paradoxes such as that recounted above do little harm. This is because, fortunately, people promptly set aside in an actual adjustment situation the reasoning and the conclusions of some piously accepted verbal systems. They act instead in a way which experience has shown to produce the desired results. Perhaps nobody, if pursued by a mad dog, would allow the logic of Zeno's paradox to govern his behavior. In an expanding secondary group society, however, men are expected to react with equal intelligence to situations of which they can have no first hand experience and regarding which, therefore, they must adjust on the basis of symbols alone. In such situations it is clearly of vast importance that our symbols and rules of logic should correspond closely to the actual events.

We shall mention later in this chapter examples of how verbal dichotomies and other conventions block scientific inquiry in the contemporary world. But the importance of a correspondence between actual events and our symbolic system is not confined to the field of science. Personal, community, and international relations constantly reflect the tensions resulting from an inadequate symbolic system of communication. Whole nations frequently fall upon each other with great ferocity because of word-systems or ideologies through which they attribute to each other characteristics, "motives," and behaviors entirely fantastic and demonstrably devoid of foundation in fact. Untold nervous energy, time, and natural resources are wasted in warfare upon, or protection against, entirely imaginary monsters conjured up by words. Widespread mental disorders result from constantly finding the world different from the word-maps upon which we rely for guidance to adjustments. Social problems cannot be solved as long as they are stated in terms as primitive and unrealistic as those which attributed diseases to demons and witches.

The survival in sociology of an approach which has long since been discarded in other sciences is due largely to the type of symbolic equipment today prevalent among social scientists. They are correspondingly inadequately equipped with the type of vocabulary and rules of symbolic manipulation which would permit analysis of the current social situation in other terms than the personalities of Dictators, Capitalism, Fascism, Democracy, Communism, Labor, and other such categories. As long as "statesmen" and leaders, not to mention scholars, waste their time tilting at these windmill-symbols, we can expect no better results than blood-letting yielded as a cure for disease. This approach yields nothing toward the understanding of that moving equilibrium of forces which constitute the maximum possible adjustment in either the biosphere or of other aspects of the cosmos.

We have emphasized in the first chapter that the immediate data of all science are symbols which represent the relationships and behavior of that aspect of the universe which we have undertaken to study. These symbols correspond to neuro-muscular sets or covert neural behavior of some kind in the human organism. The sets have been formed as a result of responses to situations. The symbols subsequently serve as substitute stimuli for these situations. When these sets, namely our verbal mechanisms and symbols, correspond closely to the conditions to which we must adjust, they greatly facilitate our adjustments. For example, a map is a highly valuable symbolic representation provided its pattern, order, and sequences correspond to the actual terrain [4] over which we must travel. It is a corresponding handicap, if it fails to indicate where the rivers and the mountains are, if it confuses the order in which they occur, or otherwise fails to correspond to the conditions to which we must adjust. Sometimes a local map which may be adequate for most kinds of travel within its own borders turns out to be very misleading for traveling beyond its borders. In the same way the verbal systems and orientations of a primitive primary group society may turn out to be grossly inadequate in a national or world society of secondary group relationships.

In addition to symbols representing situations, rules for the manipulation of these symbols, namely logic, are obviously necessary. The dominating system of both symbols and logic according to which Western man has attempted to orient himself in the social world is the Aristotelian laws of thought laid down some 2300 years ago.[5] Physical science has gradually abandoned these rules of mental procedure but the social sciences still hold to them. One of the reasons for their popularity is the clean-cut dichotomies which they set up.[6] Propositions are either true or false, things are either right or wrong, and so forth in all matters. This principle resulted in dichotomizing nicely the facts of experience into mutually exclusive compartments, which have for centuries handicapped thinking by setting up categories assumed to be inherent in the universe and holding to them regardless of how badly they served the solution of the problems at hand.[7] The absence of a mathematical technic, such as the calculus, for dealing with gradations, modes, and rates of change was undoubtedly largely responsible for the static and rigid symbolic system which the Greeks devised, and which it has been necessary to abandon in the physical sciences.

Illustrations of the prominent but mischievous role which these dichotomies have played in the history of human thought are too well-known to require more than mention. For example: (1) The induction-deduction controversy is, in the light of modern psychology, simply obsolete. (2) The heredity-environment controversy is another case in point.[8] (3) Further illustrations are found in many of the arguments regarding structure *versus* function, organization *versus* process, form *versus* activity, etc. What is overlooked is that a structure is merely a persistent function while a function is merely a series of changing structures.[9] (4) The arguments about case studies *versus* statistical method likewise disappear upon the reflection that all statistics necessarily consist of cases and that therefore there can be no antithesis or mutual exclusiveness between the two methods. The scientific import of the most thorough genetic or case or configuration analysis, on the other hand, lies in the demonstrability of its generality. The attempt to contrast quantitative technics with theory is likewise fallacious, because quantitative approaches may be as theoretical as any others.

The best general illustration of the phenomenon here under consideration, namely, the necessity of developing new symbolic technics to deal with expanding experience and new situations, is, of course, furnished by the history of the successive intellectual revolutions that mark the epochs of science. The milestones marked by Galileo, Newton, Lobatchewsky, and Einstein are common knowledge. More recently the idea has taken hold that, whereas logic is usually assumed to be the science concerned with the phenomenon of thought in general, actually this is the province of psychology.[10] Logic from this point of view becomes merely the rules by which we deal with the data of logic, namely, words. This in turn means that the postulates and rules constituting a system of logic may be indefinitely varied so as to be compatible with our observations. In short, any system of logic is justifiable or true if it provides a set of postulates which are internally consistent, that is, from which propositions can be deduced without contradiction. It is precisely this practice which has marked the great epochs of science. The Euclidian geometry set it down as an axiom that *only one* straight line can be drawn through a given point parallel to a given straight line. Lobatchewsky chose to postulate that *more than one* such line can be drawn,[11] and on this axiom proceeded to evolve what has come down to us as non-Euclidian geometry. Riemann in turn chose to postulate that *no* parallel line at all can be drawn parallel to a given line—a procedure which to the conventionally minded is simply false. Yet it was by proceeding on the Riemannian postulate that Einstein evolved the relativity theory. Each of these developments resulted from the difficulty of forcing increasingly adequate observations into the then existing verbal schemes. The new orientations provided a more adequate intellectual chart according to which mental operations could proceed without contradicting the concrete observations of life. I recite these facts not to prove that similar departures *must* be undertaken in the social sciences, but to suggest that it is one legitimate way out of an impasse, if, and only if, it serves to speed us toward the generaly accepted goal. In the meantime, we may profitably ponder the words of R. B. Winn when he says:

"Most words are like small vessels with constantly changing contents. Life does not wait for adjustments in language, but seeks to give an immediate solution to its most imperative needs and interests. . . . Consequently, there comes every once in a while a moment when traditional meanings become so overgrown with the moss of ages that they stand as a handicap for clear thinking. Then it is advisable not to continue studies along customary lines, but rather to make a determined effort toward an analysis of basic concepts in the Cartesian fashion—by purging our minds of all the accumulated presuppositions, by undertaking a re-examination of meanings, by unlearning and re-learning." (*"Is Nature Rational?" Philosophy of Science, VI, July, 1939, p. 285.*)

B. Quantitative Symbols and Methods

THE SYMBOLS MAN USES at first to represent the world are oral, and very little scientific development is possible as long as this is true. Many of the things that scientists wish to communicate simply cannot be adequately transmitted through oral language. The structure of the idea which scientists must communicate is so complex that it cannot be matched in a succession of acoustic stimuli. Consequently, the language of science must increasingly consist of written graphic symbols, which provide an enduring instead of an immediately vanishing stimulus, and offer possibilities of arrangement (tabulation, etc.) that cannot be communicated in oral language.[12] In devising written symbols, the tendency in science is to develop, as soon as possible, special symbols representing highly abstract, standardized, and ordered responses called quantitative terms instead of the highly emotionally charged words employed in everyday common-sense communication. The indefiniteness of meaning of such symbols as "many," "much," "more," "few," "less," "least" as well as avowedly "qualitative" terms such as "good," "bad," "symmetrical," "level," "heavy," "light," etc., led to the invention of numbers systems and the symbolic division of various subject-matters into *units* and scales, which are highly standardized and readily verifiable response categories.

The growing incompatibility of the symbolic system referred to above has already, as previously noted, led to its abandonment in the more advanced physical sciences and the substitution of another set of symbols and manipulatory systems. In the social sciences this transition remains largely to be accomplished. Its first steps are (1) the selection of significant categories [13] representing aspects of behavior and (2) their clear definition in terms that lend themselves to operational representations of relationships. Only if one leaves a record of the operations which one goes through in registering an observation can others verify the report.

C. "Understanding," "Insight," and Other Mystical "Methods"

IN THIS CONNECTION a common misapprehension should be corrected. I refer to the attempt, still more or less current in the social sciences, to contrast statistical, quantitative, and mathematical methods on the one hand and a method called the method of "intuition," "understanding," and "insight" on the other. The error lies in overlooking that insight and understanding are the ends at which all methods aim, rather than methods in themselves. Quantitative technics are merely the more refined, easily-used tools by which we gain insight and understanding.[14] No one has to my knowledge ever questioned the importance of the latter in all scientific endeavor. Eloquent defenses of insight and understanding, therefore, merely draw a red herring across the trail of the real question, namely: What are the methods of attaining understanding and insight? [15] We want an objective description of the *technic*. The answer to this demand in some quarters is to wear one's collar backwards, to gaze into crystals or tea cups, or to go into a trance. While being duly impressed with the remarkable results of these technics, the hardier minds in every field have always demanded a more detailed description of the steps in the procedure. Some of the abler magicians, such as Houdini have acceded to this demand by describing their technics in verifiable terms. Since verification by other qualified minds is the essence of scientific knowledge, the progress of science has been characterized by increasingly searching demands that the author of a generalization specify the steps by which he reached it.

Take, for example, the phenomenon of prediction. In prescientific terminology it is called prevision and is generally conceded to represent the highest measure of insight. Is there any *scientifically accredited* way of predicting, except in terms of probability based on past observations? The whole argument is a confusion of language. Statisticians themselves fall into the confusion when they point out that the technic of correlation must be used with understanding, logic, reason, etc. They overlook that the understanding, reason, and logic which they properly advocate is itself a method, a technic, of some kind. In fact, the insight and the understanding which we seek is to be achieved only by further correlation—formal or informal. Correlation is not merely the name of a certain statistical operation invented by Karl Pearson. It is, as the dictionary says, "the act of bringing under relations of union, correspondence or interaction; also, the conceiving of two or more things as related." [16] As such, it is a method used as frequently by other people as by statisticians. Misuse of certain specific correlation technics for purposes for which they are not adapted is, of course, common, and nobody defends such errors, least of all the statisticians. At the same time, formal correlation is no more frequently erroneous than the informal correlations which everyone practices. To attack correlation and quantitative technics in general, because of numerous faulty examples of their application, is a flagrant case of throwing out the baby with the bath.

D. The Importance of Informal Quantitative Methods

AT THIS POINT my analysis will be challenged on the ground that I interpret the meaning of statistics and quantitative methods too broadly. The current idea seems to be that if one uses pencil and paper, especially squared paper, and if one uses numerical symbols, especially Arabic notation, one is using quantitative methods. If, however, one discusses masses of data with concepts of "more" or "less" instead of formal numbers, and if one indulges in the most complicated correlations but without algebraic symbols, then one is *not* using quantitative methods.

A striking illustration from a recent book by a prominent sociologist will make the point clear. After a discussion of the lamentable limitations of statistical methods, the author appends this remarkable footnote: "Wherever the statistical method definitely gains the ascendency, the number of students of a high intellectual level who are attracted to sociology tends to fall off considerably." [17]

In short, this author finally reverts to a statistical proof of the deplorable effects of statistics. It must be clear that the only operations as a result of which one could make the statement that, as statistical methods gain ascendency, high-caliber students decrease in numbers, would be (1) to measure the degrees of relative intelligence of students; (2) to measure the quantitative variations in registrations of the better students in different sociology departments; (3) to measure the degree to which quantitative methods dominate the departments; and (4) to correlate the last two factors. The statement is an excellent example of so-called nonquantitative technics and suggests the reason for their popularity. The measurement of the factors here involved is a serious and difficult business. The generalization as quoted above was the result of a few strokes of the pen. In short, what the critics of the better quantitative methods seem to prefer is informal, impressionistic, and imaginary statistics supporting their prejudices.

The surprising implication by other sociologists that Darwin did not use quantitative methods seems to rest on a somewhat similar misunderstanding.[18] The assumption seems to be that because the *Origin of Species* contains no tables, therefore Darwin did not use quantitative methods. The patient accumulation of thousands of cases, the painstaking classification of them, the recording of the proportion of cases supporting an hypothesis and the proportion contradicting it—all this apparently does not come within the definition of quantitative methods as understood by these writers. I am not here interested in entering into a dispute about the correctness of this definition or of my own, which is much broader. I am interested only in making the point that, if such limitations exist in the definition of quantitative methods on the part of those who find the methods of little value, I am not surprised at their conclusion. But it must be clear that, if the distinction between quantitative and nonquantitative technics is to have any significance, we must take the position that a procedure is none the less quantitative or statistical if the operation is carried on without algebraic symbols or with concepts of *more* and *less* instead of with formal or exact numbers.[19] It may be alleged that this is an attempt to break down the distinction between the quantitative and the nonquantitative. That is precisely what I am interested in doing, especially in so far as it is attempted to distinguish them solely on the basis of the formality with which they are carried out.

Objectification of the technic of generalization invariably involves quantification.

E. *The Quantitative Nature of All Scientific Generalization*

THE ABOVE CONCLUSION directly raises the question as to whether scientific generalization is always and necessarily quantitative. I contend that it is. Those who find otherwise must mean something different by the term *generalization,* and they have failed to explain in operational terms what they do mean by it. I mean by the verb *generalize* the process of determining from less than all the relevant data the probable prevalence in a universe of a given datum or configuration of data. I mean by the noun *generalization* a statement arrived at by the above process. That is, I define the concept in terms of the operations by which I arrive at it, in conformity with the accepted requirements of science.[20] Is this or is it not what every scientist today means by generalization? If this definition is accepted, the question as to whether all scientific generalization is necessarily quantitative at once disappears, for quantification is implicit in the definition. If this definition is not accepted, let us have some other definition. But let us have it in operational terms, i.e., in terms of the steps involved in arriving at it. If it cannot be so defined, all argument as to its nature again disappears, as anything said by an individual regarding his private mental operations must necessarily be accepted as final and not subject to check, and therefore outside the pale of science.

As a matter of fact, I think the definition of generalization I have given above is what everyone means by the term. Those who fail to recognize it as such are simply misled by the informality with which the process is carried out, as I have illustrated above. The delusion that a scientific generalization may be drawn from a single case seems to be due to the fact that sometimes a single case happens to illustrate, typify, or coincide with the facts as stated in a generalization. This is apparently at the root of such a statement as the following: "If one perceives a single case correctly, he can generalize from that instance." [21] We are left without any operational clue as to how to perceive correctly or how to determine the correctness of a perception. Actually, of course, we say a perception is "correct" when other qualified observers confirm our report on an observation. But even when this agreement of perceptions of a single case has been established, on what possible logical grounds may one postulate that the datum or configuration of data is present more generally in the universe? There are no grounds whatever for such an assumption in the absence of further observations of additional instances.

The use of the word "correctly" above is a striking illustration of how terms of this kind frustrate thinking in the social sciences. The author clearly uses it to *mean* an observation which (1) *has been* confirmed by other qualified observers and (2) *would be* found to hold for the whole universe under consideration. In short, he jumps over the operational steps implied in the words "perceiving correctly" and thus reaches the conclusion that there are no such describable steps, but that the conclusion is "directly" revealed through the alchemy of the mind. It is this kind of verbal magic which has compelled science to insist on the operational definition of its concepts. Of course, I distinguish between what I have defined as a scientific generalization and an hypothesis, although they differ only with respect to the adequacy of the data on which they rest. Thus, the statement criticized above and such contentions as Brown's that laws precede their demonstrations confuse hypothesis with scientific law.[22]

While the author quoted above avoids giving any instructions as to how to perceive with that "correctness" which will permit us to generalize from a single case, he does essay directions as to how "we may proceed to obtain insight," and Karl Pearson himself could not improve upon them. For here it is set down categorically that *"in order to perceive with insight,"* we must engage in (1) "direct study of human and interhuman behavior," (2) study of symbols supposed to stand for such behavior, and (3) "sympathetic penetration." [23] In short, insight is not itself the method or even the beginning of the process but the result of some very mundane procedures many of the details of which in their more refined and systematic form may be found in any good text on statistics. This is what I mean by an operational definition of insight as compared with such exhortations as "try to see how data arrange themselves"; "experience phenomena with insight"; "we must look at events until they become luminous." [24] For commentary on these verbal gyrations, it would be impossible to improve on the same author's own remarks two pages later on some other matter. "An unfortunate circumstance," he says, "is that communication often breaks down, so that one acquires names without their attendant perceptual patterns. There is abundant evidence in sociological literature that many of our colleagues have learned words without perceiving processes, so that they literally do not know what they are talking about." [25]

I conclude that the notion that a scientific generalization can be drawn from a single case arises from a failure to define concepts in operational terms. Further illustration of the same confusion is found in certain current discussions of causation. Thus Köhler says: "Once more I must point out that our feeling of something naturally dependent upon something else does not refer to a correlation, or a highly constant togetherness *as such,* stated in terms of the external observations of a great many cases. It refers rather to an evident dynamical dependence as experienced *hic et nunc,* in one actual case." [26] The *"feeling* of something *naturally* dependent" and the *"evident* dynamic dependence" of two things as "felt" by an individual in "one actual case" is precisely what has led to some of the most preposterous generalizations in history. The fact that at other times such "feelings" from a single case have later been confirmed and found to hold generally in no way justifies us in confusing the hypothesis with the verified generalization. The latter is exactly what distinguishes science from other types of knowledge. Nor is this distinction any less clear or important because hypotheses are a proper part of the scientific method.

The above quotation from Köhler is an example of one of his postulates of Gestalt psychology. It seems to be the dismal destiny of sociology to fight the battles of psychology over again a decade or so after the issue has been settled or abandoned in the latter science. Thus, some of the questions regarding behaviorism which had their inning twenty years ago in psychology are still in the foreground of sociological discussion. It is not surprising, therefore, that some sociologists have now discovered Gestaltism and with it they are hoping to stave off both behaviorism and quantitative methods. In the meantime, alas, the Gestalters in psychology (especially the younger workers in the field) declare Gestaltism to be a form of behaviorism and frankly avow their adherence to quantitative and mathematical technics.[27] Thus Koffka says in his recent book: "In my opinion this famous antithesis of quantity and quality is not a true antithesis at all. It owes its popularity largely to a regrettable ignorance of the essence of quantity as used in physical science (p. 13) ... the quantitative, mathematical description of physical science, far from being opposed to quality, is but a particularly accurate way of representing quality (p. 14). . . . It (psychology) may be perfectly quantitative without losing its character as a qualitative science, and on the other hand . . . it may be unblushingly qualitative, knowing that *if its qualitative descriptions are correct,* it will sometime be possible to translate them into quantitative terms (p. 15)." [28] [Italics mine.] This concedes, of course, the point I have made above as to the quantitative test of the correctness of a generalization.

Even more striking is the declaration of J. F. Brown. "It may well be," he says, "in fact I think it very likely, that at best psychological analysis may only be statistical." [29]

Yet in the fact of these declarations by accredited Gestaltists a recent article in the *American Journal of Sociology* purporting to be "some methodological implications of the *Gestalt* principle of insight" has this passage: "The relationship of cause and effect usually assumes the form of a configuration in time. This theory enables us to avoid the ultimate nonsense of Pearsonian methodology, the doctrine that a statement of a causal relation is really only a statement of relative probabilities." [30] As to whether *cause, as science understands it,* is an "elementary datum of experience" which has nothing to do with relative probabilities I shall only refer to a bibliography on the subject including such names as Bohr,[31] Bertalanffy,[32] Bridgman,[33] Heisenberg,[34] Hecht,[35] and Schroedinger [36] in science, and others of equal repute in philosophy.[37] There is no question whatsoever as to what living and working scientists today mean by the word "cause," in so far as they concern themselves with it.[38] They have defined it in terms of the operations by which they arrive at it.[39]

F. Definition and Measurement

I HAVE REPEATEDLY referred to the importance in science of a clear definition of terms. This does not mean mere agreement on present terms, although even this is helpful. It means more especially (1) the selection of significant behavior-segments and (2) their representation by symbols which lend themselves to operational representation of relationships. That sociologists exhibit only slight agreement even in the use of the most common terms is a matter of common knowledge.[40] The same sociologist frequently uses the same term in various

senses in the same article. This state of affairs is not surprising, because the only way of defining anything objectively is in terms of the
operations involved. The individual sociologist seldom defines his
terms in this manner, even to himself. Most of the current terms cannot be defined operationally because they are mere verbalisms derived
from metaphysical postulates incapable of operational definition. In
other cases, the operational definition is deliberately avoided because
it would definitely circumscribe the meaning of words which are now
used to express not relations, but feelings, usually vague in meaning
but very strong in emotional significance. Rigid definition would
therefore interfere with rhetorical diction and block the release which
the latter affords. Many of the present terms are highly valued because of their familiar and reassuring sound, and are therefore not
infrequently mistaken for data, "fact" and "truth."

Failure to recognize the nature and functions of language results
in widespread misunderstandings about the applications of scientific
method to new fields. We have already illustrated the point with
reference to the phenomena of "mind," "fear" and "hate." (Chapter I.) Everywhere in the literature of sociology there is confusion between words and the things words stand for.[41] Take, for example, the
voluminous arguments over the "correct" or "true" meaning of a
word. Thus, Thurstone records his observation of certain behavior.
This behavior, explicitly defined operationally, he calls an attitude.
Whereupon his critics vigorously proclaim that this is not an attitude
at all.[42] *Attitude* is something else—and they proceed to define it not
by other operations than Thurstone's but by another series of noises,
which have an expressive function comparable to exclamations of joy
or sadness, laughter, or lyric poetry, but which have no objective
representative function at all. The metaphysician fails to recognize
this, and hence he wants to argue about the truth or falsity of his
expressions and definitions, whereas the poet or the musician contents
himself with calling his opponent's work, not true or false, but merely
bad.[43] Since the language in which such arguments are couched refers to no behavior which can be operationally defined, they are, of
course, incapable of solution.

Perhaps the best known illustration of futile quarreling over the
meaning of words instead of arbitrarily agreeing on them (which is
how they got their meaning in the first place) is the voluminous controversy over intelligence testing or more specifically whether what the

tests tested really was intelligence. Indeed, it was regarded as a *reductio ad absurdum* some years ago to accuse the testers of defining intelligence as *that which* the tests tested [44]—theoretically, an entirely defensible definition. Logically, and particularly in the logic of natural science, this is perhaps the best definition that can be given. No platitude is more common in sociology than the remark that in order to measure, we must first define, describe, or "know" what we are measuring. The statement usually passes as a self-evident fact which needs no examination.[45] That measurement *is* a way of defining, describing, and "knowing" seems to have been overlooked. If one confuses words with the things they signify and regards the process of definition as a mysterious intuitive revelation, instead of an ordered and selective way of responding to a situation, the idea of measuring anything without first defining it (in words supposed to possess some final essence), seems the height of absurdity. In the meantime, however, it happens that physical scientists have proceeded in just this manner. Since Einstein, at least, they have blatantly declared that space *is* that which is measured with a ruler; time *is* that which is measured by a clock; force *is* that which makes pointers move across dials, etc. For a couple of thousand years before Einstein, physicists, too, were of the impression that they must first "define" these "entities" before measuring them. Let the history of science bear witness to the barrenness of the quest, and to the enslavement of intelligence for some two thousand years by the persistence of this thought-pattern. Today the *definition* of force and its *measurement* turn out to be the same *operation*. Contrast the liberation and the forward strides of physics through the acceptance of the latter doctrine, namely, that things ARE *that which* evoke a certain type of human response, represented by measurement symbols.

The present futile disputation over societal measurement will undoubtedly be solved in the same way. It is granted, of course, that the concepts thus arbitrarily defined by the operations which register our responses will usually not mean the same as they did before, assuming that we retain many of the old words stripped of their vague, folklore connotations. Thus the term *attitude* would under an operational definition have a very much narrower but a more definite meaning than at present. This does not mean that all the other meanings which it now has would be denied or ignored, as seems to be assumed by the critics of this type of measurement. The *other* meanings in so far as

they are scientifically relevant would be similarly defined operationally by *other* words or symbolic devices. Each shade of meaning
would be designated by adjectives or other symbols distinguishing
them with whatever rigidity is regarded as desirable. It may be true
that "in stating a concept statistically, changes are made in it" by
which it "is so simplified as to be almost unrecognizable." [46] In the
same way the physicists' definition of the concept "horsepower" is
quite unrecognizable in terms of its folk-meaning. This "degradation"
(?) of concepts is, I fear, a necessary cost of scientific progress. Not
only will some existing sociological concepts have to be redefined or
abandoned, but others will have to be invented because there may be
at present no words for some social behavior-segments of basic
importance. [47]

G. "What" Do Scales Measure? [48]

WITH THE INVENTION of each new measuring instrument the question
always arises as to "what" it measures. The same question could, of
course, be asked with respect to the meaning of any of the words used
to designate a phenomenon prior to the development of quantitative
ways of responding to it. But in the case of folk-language symbols and
in the case of well-established measuring-devices this question is less
likely to arise because familiar words and units tend to be reified into
self-sufficient entities, and we do not feel that we need to account for
"what" they refer to except possibly by pointing, gesticulating, or en-
gaging in some other very overt and elementary form of behavior. It
is interesting to note, for example, that the term "socio-economic
status" passes readily from mouth to mouth among sociologists and
social workers on the assumption that it means the same to all. Only
when a formal and rigorously defined scale for measuring socio-
economic status is invented does the question arise as to "what" it
measures. It is doubtless true that such a scale includes some components and neglects others which each individual includes in that
complex response to which he attaches the words socio-economic
status. The scale makes us aware of this fact.

Our preference for the "qualitative" or pre-scalar use of the phrase
socio-economic status is perhaps attributable to the fact that no one
is compelled to break it up into components or to consider the rela-

tive weights he gives to each factor. The whole is a deliciously private and subjective reaction for which we are not consciously accountable to anyone. Consequently, we feel strongly that the meaning which we attach to such words, with which we designate certain stimuli, has some intrinsic validity or fitness, as when children (and others) are impressed with the peculiar fitness of the word "cold" to designate a certain degree of temperature. For people reared in the same culture and hence receiving their language-values from a fairly uniform source, there will be a certain uniformity in the use of such terms, usually sufficient to serve most primary group purposes. When we come in contact with people of different culture backgrounds and therefore with different word-meanings, we marvel at their gross misjudgment of such matters as socio-economic status, living wage, decency, freedom and so forth, and bring to bear against them emotions reserved for the stupid and the vulgar.

As science advances we find less and less interest in such questions, for example, as "what" electricity *is*. Except for certain types of philosophers, children, and other more or less semantically deranged persons (from the scientific point of view), most people find it sufficient to define what electricity is in terms of what it does. It is *that which* under certain circumstances kills people, makes trains go, flashes in the clouds, illuminates lamps, makes the hand of the voltmeter move to a certain score, etc. As social science advances we shall doubtless also find this type of answer adequate for the question as to what socio-economic status *is*. We shall be content to say that it is *that which* under certain circumstances makes people beg on streets, cringe before the local banker, behave arrogantly to the janitor, *that* status which is associated with certain kinds of houses, food, clothing, education, occupation; more specifically, we shall probably say that a person will be accorded status, i.e., people will behave toward him *according to their estimate of the probability that he will achieve* the maximum goals of socio-economic striving.[49] That is what we have meant by the term in prequantitative days; it is likely to continue to be what we mean by it under a quantitative terminology except that we shall state it in terms of a number of units on a scale. Each person will then know exactly what others who use the term mean.

In short, it is only when we have a quantitative scale for measuring socio-economic status that we can give an explicit account of what we are measuring. We can enumerate or point to the items which enter into the construction of the scale and the proportional weight which each item is allowed in the total score. This is not possible when the general dictionary definition or folk-usage is allowed to determine its meaning. We can never know whether another person means quite the same by the phrase as we do. When we try to determine this, we find ourself constructing, formally or informally, a quantitative scale.

It is not necessary to argue that such a scale as the Chapin scale, for example, takes into consideration the same items to the same degree as does a subjective rating of the socio-economic status of the inhabitants of a village by one or a dozen citizens or "participant observers" living in the village. Doubtless different observers will use a great variety of different criteria and their findings will vary accordingly. None of them can be declared either right or wrong as among themselves or as against the Chapin score. All of them are right according to their own criteria and wrong according to others. On the other hand, it is possible that a wide variety of different criteria would yield virtually the same results. If so, it is because these criteria are so highly intercorrelated among themselves that any one or a few of them can be used with equal reliability. In that case the criterion or criteria most easily observed, although itself apparently trivial and irrelevant, can be utilized as a reliable index of an intricate complex all the details of which are extremely difficult to secure. If study should reveal that a certain religious group of a certain income level always paint their houses blue, the latter would be at once an adequate index of economic status and religious belief. One of the most important problems in the construction of quantitative scales or scientific instruments in general is to discover such simple and obvious criteria which can be used as indices to the complex attitudes or behaviors we wish to measure. Such criteria can be discovered, of course, only by patient correlation of all factors which by suspicion, hunch, or guess we have any reason to believe may be significantly associated. Only by this process can we finally arrive at simple and useful instruments like the mercury thermometer or the various specific tests for certain diseases.

We must guard, then, in taking for granted or assuming a necessarily greater validity of conclusions reached through impressionistic or "participant-observer" technics as against the conclusions shown by more formal methods and instruments. Disagreement between the two merely indicates the desirability of *further investigation,* not that because the scale disagrees with our impressions the former is *ipso facto* wrong or less useful. In the end, one result and one method will be declared preferable on the basis of certain practical results it yields. But it is interesting to note that in our adjustments to "physical" phenomena we have become reconciled to set aside the judgment of our unaided senses in favor of the conclusions of instruments; while in our societal adjustments the presumption is still strongly in favor of the greater validity of uncorrected intuitive impressions. This *may* merely indicate that instruments for societal observation are as yet actually inferior to "common sense." At the same time, the knowledge of the limitations of our unaided senses which the other sciences have revealed suggests that the subtleties of societal phenomena call for even more refined instruments and technics of observation, thought, and analysis.

The problems of more objective symbols and of measurement are not, therefore, academic questions of preference or mere attempts to imitate the relatively highly developed sciences. These problems will thrust themselves upon our attention as soon as we attempt to improve upon the accuracy of our adjustments to a changing world. There exists today a large body of common-sense generalizations about alleged uniformities in societal behavior. This body of knowledge forms the basis of our present adjustments and they are useful not only as guides to conduct but as hypotheses for further study. To point out the limitations of these generalizations and the necessary approach to their improvement is in no sense a denial of their usefulness or of the contributions of those who have developed this knowledge to its present stage. The adages and proverbs of folklore and the pronouncements of present day journalists and sociologists, ranging from local beliefs to generalizations of cosmic scope, are probably far more numerous, varied, and generally useful than common-sense generalizations in any other field. But they are especially defective in two very important respects: They do not indicate (1) under *what conditions* these generalizations are true, and (2) to *what degree* they are true under these conditions. Until we can answer these two questions with greater accuracy than is now possible, the "principles" of sociology cannot be said to be either scientific or generally useful.

It is here that the insistent and important problem of measurement arises. The degree to which a generalization is true must always be especially important in sociology because of our inability to achieve (for the present, at least) the more perfect laboratory controls. This problem implies its own answer, namely, measurement. We are *compelled* to deal with measurement in sociology because it is implicit in that testing and verification of hypotheses which everyone admits is the *sine qua non* of natural science. Furthermore, the chief source of enlightening new theories in sociology as in other fields is likely to be the by-product of just such testing of present hypotheses. The main stimulus to the creation of a new theory is the demonstration of the inadequacy of the old. The bulk of scientific research must always consist of the testing of the currently accepted "principles" and their modification in the light of that more adequate determination of fact, which is measurement.

Acceptance of the above reasoning does not, of course, constitute any solution of the concrete problems of measurement in the social sciences. The serious and difficult task of developing useful and valid measuring scales still remains. We only remove by the above reasoning the logical prohibition which declares their development to be impossible. The protracted work by which measuring instruments have been invented and perfected in the physical sciences remains to be done in sociology. How long did it take, for example, to develop the common yardstick, not to mention technics of measuring a millionth of an inch? Such work must be performed as a condition of progress. In the meantime, the theoretical rationale here presented is demanded both as an hypothesis on which to work and as a justification for devoting ourselves to the slow and undramatic labor upon technology which always has been and always will be the principal condition of scientific progress in all fields.

H. Some Theoretical Problems in the Measurement of Societal Phenomena

WHILE THERE IS at present considerable disagreement as to the proper province of measurement in sociology, everyone probably admits that one of the most essential requirements for further advance is a more objective selection and definition of the behavior-segments that we regard as basic or at least important in this field. I have argued above that the problem of definition is inseparable from the problem of measurement, and, further, that social measurements can and do fulfill the same logical requirements as measurements in the other sciences. Since the point is a basic one and since some highly qualified people who have themselves made noteworthy contributions to the development of sociological and psychological measuring devices find theoretical difficulties in the position I have taken, it is desirable to consider here some of the objections that have been raised.

Perhaps the subtlest is that which finds certain things intrinsically measurable while others are regarded as measurable only in a secondary or less fundamental sense. It is contended, for example, that whereas weight, distance, time, or force are phenomena fundamentally and truly measurable, temperature, hardness, and density are measurable only in an ordinal or secondary sense, and that attitudes, aptitudes, ability, or intelligence are not measurable in either sense, if at all.[50]

For purposes of this discussion we shall adopt the most restricted definition of measurement, namely, that which requires scalar units, which are additive and interchangeable as units. In short, we shall accept the definition which everyone admits characterizes the measurement of such phenomena as weight, distance, and time. On this basis, Nagel finds density not in the same sense measurable as weight. Many others find that such devices as Thurstone's attitude scales are not of the same logical class as measuring scales of weight, time, space, etc. Since the argument is basically the same in each case, let us first examine Nagel's contention that "there is no clear sense in which two liquids equally dense could be added to produce a liquid twice as dense." [51] This is not a question of sociological measurement at all, but it illustrates the basic fallacy involved in most objections to sociological measurement. It is significant to note also that the concept of density and its measurement is a much more recent and, therefore, unfamiliar development than the measurement of weight.

We pointed out in Chapter I that the immediate data of science are symbols. It follows that we never actually measure or weigh either liquids or bricks in all their aspects, i.e., in all the respects in which they are capable of evoking responses. We respond selectively to some one aspect, property, or quality at a time. It may be weight, mass, color, density, hardness, sweetness, malodorousness, radicalism, or what not. This response, symbolized, is the immediate datum for science. We devise various means of *ordering* successive or numerous responses of the same kind. As between two of them we say that one is better, pleasanter, greater, harder, sweeter, or brighter than the other. Among larger numbers we arrange them in series according to the pressure sensations they evoke in us, the tactile resistance they offer, the visual space they occupy, or their behavior manifested to us through any other of our senses.

The next step in formalizing the process is to interject a mechanical device between our elementary original responses and *that which* evokes the response. For example, instead of gauging verbally ("heavier," "lighter,") the relative weights of two bricks by the directly experienced pressure sensations felt by balancing one in each hand, we may construct a balance (according to principles established previously by similar processes) and draw our conclusions about the weight of the two objects from visual instead of tactile stimuli, i.e., the balancing of a beam or the position of a pointer on a calibrated dial.

Now all the steps (operations) in the construction and calibration of this device are essential considerations in interpreting its behavior as a measurement of weight.[52] But to all who are familiar with and accept the validity of these steps, the beam is accepted as a device for *standardizing responses* and securing more perfect agreement among a number of observers. The units, whether of mass, weight, color, density, hardness, or anything else, are not "parts" or "fractions" of any two bricks or of bricks in general.[53] They are abstractions, [54] *symbols of magnitude. Magnitude* is the name of a selective response. *Units* of magnitude are symbols invented to represent various kinds (gradations) of magnitude responses. As such, units of a given scale are *per se* interchangeable and may be subjected to any mathematical manipulation considered meaningful, regardless of what phenomena in a given case they may refer to. Thus, we may not add bricks and hogs; but *pounds,* i.e., abstractions called *weight magnitudes, of bricks and hogs* may be added. Likewise, it is perfectly true that "there is no clear sense in which two *liquids* equally dense could be added to produce a liquid twice as dense." [55] Only *magnitudes* (abstractions) are ever added (mathematically).[56] Two equal units of density-magnitude can assuredly be added and a new density-magnitude twice as great can be secured. The familiarity of the operations with which we carry out some measurements has caused us to believe that others, less familiar and formal, involve other logical (or "fundamental") principles. The same reasoning will hold for the alleged differences in "direct" measurability of such phenomena as hardness and temperature as compared to weight.

I. Summary of Fallacious Assumptions Regarding Measurement

LET ME NOW summarize my criticism of the four principal thought-ways regarding the measurability of different types of phenomena, and the resulting impasse in social research.

1.   The main reason for asserting that some things are measurable while others are not is the implicit assumption that measurement is not a way of defining things, but is a process which can be carried out only after the "thing" to be measured has been defined. This, of course, implies in turn some kind of "existences" of phenomena as "common essences." As has been repeatedly pointed out above, natural science cannot deal with these hypothetical "entities" but must confine itself to the data of human responses, however evoked.

2.   Under this restriction the postulation of some units as "natural" and others as "artificial" must also be abandoned. Thus, one able writer says that "a person is a natural unit in measuring population"; whereas, degrees, calories, and ergs, not to mention the units of attitude scales, are artificial.[57] By what postulate can this distinction be made? To distinguish "natural" from "artificial" units we must postulate that some units have inherent existence as "common essences" in the universe, whereas others are the constructs of man's convenience —a way of responding to a situation symbolically represented. It is my contention that *all* units are of the latter character. The former postulate is implicit or explicit in nearly all social sciences today. The social sciences are hopelessly entangled in the notion that some phenomena are "directly" known and are "material," as contrasted with "mental" and "spiritual" phenomena. Such postulates are not only incompatible with modern science; they completely block further systematic advancement of knowledge in the social field. These assumptions lead to endless, wearisome, and completely futile discussions of

the relative "realities" of the individual, of society, of culture, and of "physical" things. The only escape from the impasse is to do what physics has done with respect to its units, namely, recognize that they are all linguistic constructs ("artificial") symbolizing human responses to aspects of the universe relevant to particular problems which man faces.

Closely related to the above misconception of the nature of scientific units is that which holds "man" to be the "natural" unit of sociology. This is analogous to saying that earth, air, fire, or water are the "natural" units of physics. But physics no longer attempts to operate with such units. The units of physics are abstractions—symbols standing for *our responses* to certain situations or phenomena. The "nature" of these phenomena we infer from our responses. All questions of naturalness, artificiality, or "existence" of the units are completely obsolete because units are *defined* as symbols of our responses to *that which* evokes them.[58] The assumption of the naturalness or "existence" of some units as against the artificiality and abstractness (non-existence) of others is a clear Aristotelian survival incompatible with modern natural science and is being rapidly abandoned. All that can be said is that "man" is a convenient unit for certain crude purposes just as certain commonplace physical adjustments are made by regarding tables, chairs, and stones as units. But what was the state of the physical sciences while these natural, convenient, and obvious units, or even earth, air, fire, and water, were regarded as the "units"?

3. A third important reason for the apparent difference between social and physical units and measurements is the implicit or explicit assumption that we measure the *behavior* of some things, but the *being, quality,* or *quantity* of others. The latter set of words have, of course, been reified into things, although they actually stand only for human responses. Take, for example, the statement that degrees, calories, and ergs are "artificial" units because here *"effects produced* constitute units in the indices of the *thing to be measured."* [59] [Italics mine.] The *unit* "man" is *likewise* an *"effect produced"*—upon the sense organs of the perceiver. It is only when there is relative stability and uniformity in the sensory responses of numerous competent observers that we can postulate either his existence or his unitary nature with reference to the attendant situation to which we also respond. Degrees, calories, ergs, are words *symbolizing sensory responses.*

"Man" is just another such word, but a very crude one because it leaves to the context the task of determining what aspect of "man" (always implicit) is meant, instead of denoting it specifically. The character of the stimuli that evoked any of these responses is postulated from inferences from these responses. Our alleged "knowledge" of the phenomena that evoke our responses consist of just such inferences.

4. Finally, there is the problem of the alleged physical "counterparts" of some scales or measures as compared with others. This is the question of the "objective existence" and "meaning" of the units of sociological scales and is probably adequately covered by the preceding discussion. Thus, Kirkpatrick says that when a scale value of 5.7 is assigned to a certain statement on a Thurstone scale "the number 5.7 is not a multiple of any objective unit." [60] This seems to contradict his own earlier concessions to the position advanced in the present volume and to confuse the meaning of his own terms. He has previously admitted that "all units are perceptually and conceptually defined by human beings and have only relative interchangeability." [61] He would presumably further admit that "objectivity" is a postulate resting solely on the confirmatory response of numerous qualified observers. If so, a unit (i.e., a spatial marking) on a Thurstone scale is "physical," "observable," manipulable, and "objective" in precisely the same sense that a gram is. With respect to interchangeability he says: "Let it be assumed that a score on a Thurstone scale is five. The question arises 'five what?' The answer is five intervals on an eleven point scale which were supposedly equal appearing to judges reared in a particular culture." [62] This is precisely the only legitimate answer that can be made to a corresponding inquiry as to the meaning of the following question: "Let it be assumed that a 'score' on the beam or dial of a druggists' scale is 5. Five what? Five intervals on (say) a hundred point scale, supposedly equal in the judgment of those who calibrated the scale." [63] Kirkpatrick goes on to say: "The equal appearing unit [in the Thurstone scale] had no direct physical counterpart in the sense that a brass gram weight corresponds to the idea of a gram as a unit rather than as a symbol like the word 'gram.' " [64] This is a clear case of postulating "existence" of brass *gram weights* as "common essences" and therefore finding them "different" from the "existence" (behavior) which must by the same logic be postulated (by inference) for the behavior-in-environment *represented by* the statements originally sorted by Thurstone's judges.

Brass gram weights or the "idea of a gram as a unit" do not exist
for science or knowledge prior to man's ordered reactions to kines-
thetic pressure sensations. When he *has* such sensations he symbolizes
them, perhaps first by sounds (words), perhaps then by pebbles, or
other objects arranged in order of size, since volume in this case has
been observed to correlate highly with intensity of pressure sensations.
He may then, on account of the high observed correlation between
volume and weight in certain material, proceed to divide metals into
equal volumes and by combining them represent mathematical interchangeability and other convenient manipulatory effects. He may further represent all these operations graphically.

Now the raw material of a Thurstone scale on (say) economic
radicalism is certain behaviors-in-environment of human beings which
are observed by themselves or by others. In attitude scales, certain behavior ("the physical counterpart") has been observed and has been
symbolized by words and statements which, in writing, have been
collected. Judges whose sensory apparatus and reaction tendencies
are similar to those of the original reagents (i.e., those whose behavior is described by the original statements), arrange these statements (*they* are now the physical counterparts) into series, of more
and less, of a quality (radicalism) which they indicate. A scale with
arbitrary divisions representing an average of the reactions (serial
placements) of the judges is then arranged. These divisions or units
are then represented spatially on paper, or could be constructed of
brass and be arranged in any order desired. When arranged they are
always numbered successively by agreement, from left to right, as are
other scales, dials, etc. What are the "physical counterparts" of a
score on an attitude test? Today we answer that question by saying
that a score of (say) 4 on a test designed to measure attitudes toward
Negroes denotes the attitude of people who, for example, answer
Question 1 in the affirmative and Question 10 in the negative, etc.,
and *only* the attitude of the people so responding. This is just as
definitely a "physical counterpart" as can be assigned to a point on
any "physical" scale.

If, by the procedure described, one person scores 5 and another
10,[65] one may be called "twice" as radical as the other with precisely
the same logic which declares that one stone is twice as heavy as
another. The latter statement means that we have abstracted weight-
quality out of a total complex of some kind and represented the ab-

straction by symbols of some kind, in this case, units-on-a-scale. In terms *of this scale,* one stone is twice as heavy as another, and in no other "inherent," "fundamental" sense. In either case, it is a meaningful statement only to people who accept the symbolic operation involved. Note that in the above illustration, I have first defined radicalism in terms of the scores-on-a-scale, just as weight must be so defined in terms of its scale.[66] It is unnecessary to argue whether what is tested is "really" an attitude, because attitude is defined as *that behavior* evoked by this test. It is likewise futile to argue whether a certain behavior considered in a test is "really" radical. For the constructors of the test and the scale agree to *call* it radical. It is, therefore, also unnecessary to argue whether the statement that one individual is twice as radical as another is "comparable," "similar," and as logically defensible as the statement that one stone is twice as heavy as another, because in terms of the units of the two scales (both of which assume an arbitrary, rational origin) one is obviously twice the other in both cases. Controversy over such matters illustrates the hopeless current confusion of linguistic and logical constructs with metaphysical postulates of existences, essences, beings, etc. The great contribution of relativity theory was to expose this confusion. Hence its vast significance for the social as well as the physical sciences.

It has been my main interest in this section to emphasize and illustrate the tendency to overlook the basic nature of language units, knowledge, and logic. I have confined myself to illustrations of only a few of the fallacious thoughtways in sociology. But most of them derive from the same basic considerations. We assume too lightly that the knowledge more familiar to us has an inherency in the universe instead of being only well-established and therefore more uniform ways of responding. We *overlook* the postulates of well-established thought-patterns, and either assume there are none or at least that they are self-evident, eternal, and inherent in the universe, just as the postulates of Euclidian geometry. Aristotelian physics and logic, and every basic postulate of folk-belief has been taken for granted. Now all postulates must and should be taken for granted. But we must remember that we do *take* them for granted and that they are not divinely imposed on us. Otherwise, we handicap ourselves fatally in the development of new advances in science which frequently require new postulates. If sociologists were compelled to make *explicit* the postulates which are *implicit* in their present orientation, they would speak with less condescension about the thought-ways of their primitive ancestors.

If the above diagnosis is in the main a correct characterization of the present situation in sociology (and in the other social sciences as well) the following general approach is indicated.[67]

1. A survey of the present body of sociological theory and "principles" (a) to sift out the matter which seems most relevant to basic problems, and (b) to scrutinize and render explicit the postulates upon which present theory and principles are based.

2. A survey of the terms at present in common use and by fairly common agreement admitted to represent the phenomena of special interest to sociology.

3. Agreement on the definition of these terms in operational language.[68]

4. The formulation, on the basis of the above work, of a comprehensive theory fulfilling as nearly as possible the generally accepted requirements of a scientific theory.

This program does not contemplate, it should be noted, any wholesale abandonment of any existing sociological theory, principles or empirical research without the most careful consideration of its possible value in whole or in part. A new scheme or system spun out of thin idealistic air, the aura of other sciences, or the pronouncements of Aristotle, Marx, Aquinas, and Einstein is not contemplated. All of these, and others, will, however, be considered as legitimate sources of suggestions as to the meaningful arrangements of the considerable body of empirical and other research upon which present sociology rests. Necessarily, the principal source of any new formulation will be the existing body of sociological theory and fact. The amorphous mass of tangible results of research must be assembled around the generalizations upon which these researches may conceivably be supposed to bear. The more specific generalizations must then be arranged under the broader principles which they seem to support. This procedure will doubtless reveal vast gaps in sociological knowledge. But the first step in filling a gap is locating it as definitely as possible. Further research can then be centered upon the crucial sectors—those problems the solution of which is a prerequisite for further advance. Such research will also serve as a constant check on the postulates and the theory upon which we proceed. "If the deductions involve conditions of observation which are now impossible of attainment, the theory is metaphysical rather than scientific; and if the deduced phenomenon is not observed when the conditions are fulfilled, the theory is false." [69] From the cumulative results of research based upon a coherent set of postulates and directed at clearly stated hypotheses there should emerge an increasingly adequate set of postulates, concepts (words), and verifiable theorems to form the basic framework of sociology.

J. Conclusion

THE PRINCIPAL THEME of this chapter was well stated by Francis Bacon several centuries ago. "There are," he said, "also idols formed by the intercourse and association of men with each other, which I call Idols of the Marketplace, on account of the commerce and consort of men there. For it is by discourse that men associate; and words are imposed according to the apprehension of the vulgar. And therefore the ill and unfit choice of words wonderfully obstructs the understanding. . . . But words plainly force and overrule the understanding, and throw all into confusion, and lead men away into numberless empty controversies and idle fancies." [70]

A great many thinkers and writers on the social sciences have been agitated over the same problem. But thus far little has been done about it. The basic vocabulary of social science, to take a political example, remains today largely what it was when Thomas Aquinas wrote his *Rule of Princes* in the thirteenth century, or when Aristotle wrote his *Politics*. In the meantime the other sciences have abandoned practically all of the words and symbolic systems of Aquinas's time. Mechanical calculating machines perform with Arabic numerals operations far beyond the imagination of the most brilliant intellect working with Roman numerals. The instruments of the physics laboratory have practically nothing in common with those of the alchemist's cellar.

We have examined in this chapter some of the reasons for this backwardness in the development of adequate symbols in the social sciences. The most commonly assigned reason is that the subtleties, complexities, and dynamic character of societal phenomena preclude the development of the more rigorously defined symbols and methods of other sciences. We have tried to show that these are the very considerations which dictate the development of precisely the kind of symbols which are declared to be inapplicable to societal phenomena. This suspicion of new symbols springs from a survival of the mystical belief in the intrinsic character and properties of words, which is so common among primitive peoples. We have here taken the view that words are, like other instruments of man, constructs of his convenience and to be judged solely by their effectiveness.

It is in this connection that we have pointed out that the technics of symbolic logic and mathematics were invented in order to remedy the hopeless inadequacy of the language of folklore as a vehicle for the description of situations at all subtle, complex, or dynamic. Measurement is merely an objectification of a procedure which has always been practiced with greater or lesser accuracy. Without quantitative units, the vocabulary required to describe the tremendously varied gradations in societal phenomena would be of such staggering proportions as to be a hopeless handicap to intellectual activity, communication, and other adjustments. The Arabic language contains about 6000 names for "camel," [71] a separate symbol for each kind and condition of camel. Imagine the situation if every size of house in a large city could be described only by a separate, noninterchangeable symbol instead of in terms of a certain *number* of stories, cubic contents, height, width, etc. Everyone complains about the variety and complexity of societal phenomena. Yet we try to describe them by using a separate word for each gradation, or at most resorting to vague qualifications of "more," "less," "some," etc. In our struggle to make increasingly fine distinctions we are constantly multiplying our words on the ground that each has its "shade of meaning." Unfortunately, the shades are frequently more apparent than the meanings.

We need instead to develop quantitative units and forms of expression so that we may utilize in the description of societal phenomena the tremendously powerful technics of mathematics which are already available. By regarding all qualitative gradations as *degrees* or *amounts* of that quality,[72] already existing numerical units and manipulating technics can be utilized in accurate and objective description of qualities and relationships. The practical task of developing scales for the quantitative expression of qualitative differences remains a major concern of the social scientist. Dodd has suggested methods by which such social "processes," as for example, those traditionally called "conflict," "accommodation," and "cooperation" may be reduced to a continuum in terms of degrees of societal tension.[73] Through such an approach, endless discussion of the definition of these and other similar terms and disagreements as to which term applies to a given situation, might be resolved.

Finally we have stressed the fundamentally quantitative nature of all scientific generalization. Whatever view one may take regarding the practical possibility of inventing valid instruments for the quantitative description of the varied gradations and relationships of societal phenomena, the quantitative requirements of scientific generalization cannot be escaped. This applies with equal validity to "case studies," "qualitative analysis," and all other supposedly nonquantitative technics. If it is desired to generalize from the most intuitional, artistic, or qualitative experience, the requirement of *other corroborative instances* of the alleged phenomenon is in science inescapable.

A coherent and consistent system of symbols corresponding closely to the world to which we have to adjust is important not only to science but also from the standpoint of mental health and practical social administration. A very large part of the environment to which men respond consists of words—spoken or written, assembled into sentences and ideologies. These word-systems are variously incorporated into so-called "material" forms such as totem poles, monuments, tablets, books, buildings, and institutional paraphernalia and behavior generally. Once language is acquired it is possible to experience just as actual and severe organic tensions on a purely linguistic ("intellectual") level as one experiences on being caught in some "physical" predicament. That is, the tensions which many people experienced under the conflicting impact of the theories of evolution and theology are, from the point of view here adopted, comparable and amenable to analysis within the same framework as the tensions experienced by a person finding his escape from a dangerous animal cut off by a precipice. The adjustment-behaviors in which the organism engages under the two situations may involve quite different parts and sequences of the organism, but the behavior may be described and explained within the same system of logic (rules of verbal manipulation).

A very large proportion of the population of many countries is today carrying on a major part of their lives in an impersonal machine culture to which they adjust according to the assumptions and rules (word-systems) of science. Another important part of their lives (linguistic and otherwise), having to do with their social adjustments, is carried on according to vitalistic, animistic, primary-group assumptions and doctrines of a bygone age. The resulting tensions, confusions, and maladjustments are everywhere evident. (See especially Chapter VIII, Sec. B, 4 of the First Edition.) Our schizoid societal behavior resides largely, we shall see, in the inadequate and inconsistent symbolic systems according to which we attempt to steer our course.[74]

Whatever views one may take of the issues discussed above, there is no doubt that, for better or for worse, the past twenty-five years have seen a remarkable development of quantitative methods in sociology. (See bibliography in note 1 below.) The estimate of one sociologist, who is himself skeptical of the advisability of the trend, may be of interest. In a paper published in 1950 on "Sociological Theory Today," Professor N. F. Timasheff says: "The school dominating present-day sociology at least in America is the neopositivist one. It is best represented in G. Lundberg's *Foundations of Sociology* (1939), in its companion volume which is S. C. Dodd's *Dimensions of Society* (1942), but also in such works as G. K. Zipf's *Human Behavior and the Principle of Least Effort* (1949), in N. Rashevsky's *Mathematical Theory of Human Relations* (1947), and in innumerable articles appearing in the sociological journals." ("Sociological Theory Today," *American Catholic Sociological Review*, XI (March, 1950), p. 26.)

I hope Timasheff is right in his conclusion that this is the dominant school. For those who, like myself, have wondered what different people mean when they use the terms "positivist" and "neopositivist," Timasheff's statement also has the virtue of more than usual definiteness in that it refers to the viewpoint contained in certain specified books which do in fact represent a common orientation. Unfortunately, Timasheff's understanding of neopositivism is at some variance not only with other definitions that are current but also with the viewpoints of some of the books that he designates as definitive works on neopositivism. Because of this uncertainty of the definition of the "school," and more especially because of the many curious associations which the term "positivism" has in many minds, I have always preferred to characterize my own viewpoint as that of *natural science* rather than attempt to identify it with any of the conventional schools of traditional philosophy, of which positivism has been one, at least since Comte. The extent to which I find Comte's doctrines compatible with my own was set forth in "Contemporary Positivism in Sociology," *American Sociological Review,* IV (February, 1939), 42-55. When I have used the words "positivism" and "operationism," I have meant generally the position of the Vienna Circle. Briefly and more specifically, I would refer to the following more recent publications of H. Feigl, "Logical Empiricism," in *Twentieth Century Philosophy,* ed. D. D. Runes (New York: Philosophical Library, 1953); "Operationism and Scientific Method," *Psychological Review,* LII (September, 1945), 250-59; "Principles and Problems of Theory Construction in Psychology," in Wayne Dennis *et al., Current Trends of Psychological Theory* (Pittsburgh: University of Pittsburgh Press, 1959). These papers, all of which appeared a decade or more after my *Foundations of Sociology* was written, are also, to me, an invaluable summary of important developments in the philosophy of science in the last twenty-five years.

K. *Notes*

1. For a recent account of quantification in both the physical and the social sciences with special reference to the history of quantification, see Harry Woolf, editor, *Quantification: A History of the Meaning of Measurement in the Natural and Social Sciences,* Bobbs-Merrill, 1961. See also Paul F. Lazarsfeld and Morris Rosenberg, editors, *The Language of Social Research: A Reader in the Methodology of the Social Sciences,* Free Press, 1955; Paul F. Lazarsfeld, editor, *Mathematical Thinking in the Social Sciences,* Free Press, 1954. Also, G. A. Lundberg, "Quantitative Methods in Sociology: 1920-1960," *Social Forces,* Vol. 39, October, 1960, pp. 19-24.

2. For illustrations see Stuart Chase, *The Tyranny of Words,* Harcourt, 1938; T. W. Arnold, *The Folklore of Capitalism,* Yale University Press, 1937.

3. See the geometric demonstration in L. Hogben, *Mathematics for the Million,* Norton, 1937, p. 89.

4. The nature of the "actual terrain" is, for adjustment purposes, relative to the organism making the adjustment. For example, any given terrain is different for man than it is for microbes which pass readily through the walls of houses or through other barriers which impede man's movements. By the same reasoning a given terrain is different for primitive and for modern man.

5. It is not necessary to become involved here in the question of whether these departures are contradictions of Aristotelian logic or merely extensions of it. (For a discussion of the subject, with references to Aristotle's works, see O. L. Reiser "Non-Aristotelian Logics," *The Monist,* XLV, Jan., 1935, pp. 100-117.) The fact seems to be that these later developments consist essentially of showing that the older systems are merely special cases of, and therefore included in, the broader postulates of Lobatchewsky, Riemann, and Einstein. I am using the term non-Aristotelian purely as a term generally (and perhaps erroneously) employed to designate these later developments. The reasoning on this subject is, therefore, in no way concerned with or dependent upon what Aristotle actually said or what is a legitimate interpretation of his remarks. A considerable number of qualified scholars, however, regard the more recent dynamic and functional viewpoints of science as so basically at variance with the thought-patterns which preceded them that the former must be regarded as really *non*-Aristotelian. (See E. T. Bell, *The Search for Truth,* Williams and Wilkins, 1934, Ch. VII; K. Lewin, *A Dynamic Theory of Personality,* McGraw-Hill, 1935, Ch. I; A. Korzybski, *Science and Sanity,* Science Press, 1933; A. F. Bentley, *Linguistic Analysis of Mathematics,* Principia Press, 1932, p. 304.)

6. The arbitrariness of this system has been exposed in the epoch-making work of Lucasiewicz and Tarski; see C. I. Lewis and C. H. Langford, *Symbolic Logic,* Century, 1932; also A. F. Bentley, *op. cit.*

7. Curiously enough, quantitative technics are by some suspected of being guilty of just this shortcoming, though the history of mathematics and statistics clearly demonstrates the opposite.

8. For elaboration of this point see G. A. Lundberg, "The Biology of Population Cycles," *Social Forces,* IX, March, 1931, pp. 405-408. Also Ch. VI of the unabridged edition and pp. 451-456.

9. L. K. Frank, "Structure, Function and Growth," *Philosophy of Science,* April, 1935, p. 213; also Alexis Carrel, "The New Cytology," *Science,* LXIII, March 20, 1931, p. 298; also G. E. Coghill, "The Neuro-Embryologic Study of Behavior: Principles, Perspective, and Aim," *Science,* LXXVIII, Aug. 18, 1933, p. 137.

10. R. Carnap, *Philosophy and Logical Syntax,* Kegan Paul, 1935, p. 34.

11. E. T. Bell, *op. cit.,* p. 216.

12. Cf. Leonard Bloomfield, "Linguistic Aspects of Science," *Philosophy of Science,* II, Oct., 1935, pp. 499-517.

13. *Categories* may be made arbitrarily mutually exclusive without imputing any discontinuity to the phenomena referred to. "Conceptual analysis permits the parts to be conceived as they are when the parts of the living whole, and not as they would be if physically isolated.... An analysis is a veritable construct of the person who makes it. The parts are not logically given in the whole. In constructing an analysis, a person builds a new—and perhaps better—way of responding to a thing—a new way of dealing with it 'mentally.'... The merits or demerits of a physical or any other type of analysis are for a scientist questions of the success they yield in predicting or controlling. (M. A. Copeland, "An Instrumental View of the Part-Whole Relation," *Journal of Philosophy,* XXIV, pp. 96-104, 1927.) (See also Ch. I, Section C, 6 of the present volume.) This point seems to be involved in the following passage from R. M. MacIver, *Society, A Textbook of Sociology,* Farrar and Rinehart, 1937, p. 476. "Social phenomena are not, like certain physical phenomena, isolable components of a situation. Social phenomena are aspects of a total non-mechanical, consciously upheld system of relationships." Later on the same page he admits however, and I think correctly, that the kind of isolability he has in mind is impossible also in "physical" situations. "We can say that land, labor, capital, and organization—to take the old categories—are all necessary to produce a steel rail, but the question how much does each produce remains not only unanswerable, but meaningless. If a number of factors are alike *necessary* to the production of a result, there can be no quantitative evaluation of their respective contributions. [How about H_2O? G. L.] And if this is true of material categories, themselves measurable, and their material products, themselves also measurable, it is *a fortiori* true of the more subtle interactions of personalities," etc. (P. 476). If the components present in any situation are reduced to units of some kind then the *number or amount of these units* present can certainly be stated. If we can say that land, labor, and capital are the components that enter into a steel rail, then we can also say how much of each of the components enter into the production of the rail, after we have reduced the components to countable units. We perceive quantitative aspects of things just as truly as we perceive other aspects of them. MacIver uses the illustration to demonstrate the shortcomings of quantitative methods in "explaining" "causation" because these "quantitative indices are merely evidences of an interaction which they do not explain." (P. 476.) I do not find that the illustration has any such implication as MacIver suggests. The "explanation" which he has in mind remains to be performed after he has named his components in any case. The statement of the quantity or degree to which each component is present greatly

facilitates that description of the relationships and interaction of the components without which his explanation is in either case not forthcoming. I accept completely MacIver's point (as I understand it) that the description of the *interaction of all the necessary factors* involved in an end result constitutes its explanation. I merely hold that mathematical formulas in quantitative terms are the most accurate way yet devised for describing just such interaction. The argument over the applicability of quantitative methods is clearly due to different conceptions of the nature of these methods.

This is further indicated, I think, by such a statement as the following: "To understand social causation, therefore, it is not enough to enumerate factors, to set them side by side, to attribute to them different weights as determinants of change. The first and essential thing is to discover the way in which the various factors are *related* to one another, the logical order within which each fall, the respective modes in which they enter into the causal process." (R. M. MacIver, *op. cit.*, p. 478.) Statistical and mathematical procedures were invented to achieve precisely these purposes and they remain the most perfect instruments thus far devised to achieve all of the above objectives. When we weight a factor we do exactly what the above quotation insists must be done; i.e., we assign it a weight on the basis of its *relevance,* its *relative influence,* and its mode of operation in an observed event. In short, the quotation seems to assume that statistics pretend somehow to be a substitute for, rather than an instrument of, analysis.

The above statement that "social phenomena are not, like certain physical phenomena, isolable components of a situation" is also a good illustration of the widespread tendency to confuse words with what they symbolize. Factoring a situation or determining its components consists of responding selectively to various aspects of a situation. It may or may not be possible to dissect the situation "physically." But by symbolizing each aspect, these symbols may be so arranged as to represent in a revealing way the interaction of the parts. (See reference to Copeland above.) Elsewhere MacIver seems to agree with this view, e.g., p. viii (*op. cit.*).

14. Even crude and inadequate quantitative technics sometimes reveal relationships which are not otherwise perceptible. (Cf. L. L. Thurstone, *The Vectors of Mind*, University of Chicago Press, 1935, p. 206.) I am here accepting the conventional usage of such words as "insight" and "understanding" as describing an adjustment achieved, namely, when our curiosity for some reason comes to rest. Later I shall show that from the operational viewpoint *understanding* and *insight* must themselves be regarded as technics. (See notes 19 and 32.)

15. "The gestalters have made much of the notion of insight, but, unfortunately, this idea has become enveloped with a kind of mysticism. It

appears to me that *insight* is only another name for a process which has long been familiar to us." (O. L. Reiser, "The Logic of Gestalt Psychology," *Psych. Rev.*, XXXVIII, July, 1931, p. 360.)

16. Funk and Wagnalls' *New Standard Dictionary*, 1931.

17. Florian Znaniecki, *The Method of Sociology*, Farrar and Rinehart, 1934, p. 235.

18. E.g., Herbert Blumer, *Amer. Jour. Sociol.*, XXXV, p. 1102.

19. "There can be no doubt," says Professor Morris R. Cohen, "that it is of the essence of scientific method that vague terms like *large* and *small*, *far* and *near*, *hot* and *cold*, etc., shall be replaced by terms made definite by measurement." (M. R. Cohen, *Reason and Nature*, Harcourt, 1931, p. 89. See also L. L. Bernard, "The Evolution of Social Consciousness and of the Social Sciences," *Psychological Review*, XXXIX, March, 1932, pp. 147-164; "The Development of Methods in Sociology," *The Monist*, XXXVIII, Apr., 1928, pp. 292-320.) The fact that a branch of chemistry is called "Qualitative Analysis" is sometimes advanced as proof that not all science is quantitative. Further investigation of this matter will soon convince the investigator of the important quantitative aspects also of this division of chemistry. See note 27 below.

20. "Let anyone examine in operational terms any popular present-day discussion of religious or moral questions to realize the magnitude of the reformation awaiting us [p. 32]. . . . I believe that many of the questions asked about social and philosophical subjects will be found to be meaningless when examined from the point of view of operations. It would doubtless conduce greatly to clarity of thought if the operational mode of thinking were adopted in all fields of inquiry as well as in the physical." (P. W. Bridgman, *The Logic of Modern Physics*, Macmillan, 1932, p. 30.)

For a consideration of the possible limitations of operationalism, see R. B. Lindsay, "A Critique of Operationalism in Physics," *Phil. of Sci.*, IV, Oct., 1937, pp. 456-470. This article does not deny the superiority of operational methods but merely raises the question as to whether science should rely *solely* upon such methods. I have no objection to the use of nonoperational concepts, if they are found useful, until the more desirable operationally defined concepts are developed in any field. The latter are, however, the goal to be sought. (See also H. Alpert, "Operational Definitions in Sociology," *Amer. Sociol. Rev.*, III, Dec., 1938, pp. 855-861.)

"The only justification for our concepts is that they serve to represent the complex of our experiences; beyond this they have no legitimacy. I am convinced that philosophers have had a harmful effect upon the progress of scientific thinking in removing certain fundamental concepts from the domain of empiricism, where they are under our control, to the intangible heights of the *a priori*." (A. Einstein, *The Meaning of Relativity*, Princeton University Press, 1923, p. 2.)

The statement "no virtuosity of technique can compensate for want of understanding" [Waller (cited below), p. 290] uses the word "understanding" in precisely the way attacked by Einstein. Understanding *is* a "virtuosity of technique," from the operational point of view.

"The older elementalistic linguistic problems of 'matter,' 'space,' and 'time' were in such a mess, due to the objectification of verbal structures, that it was useless to talk any more in the old way. He [Einstein] decided to describe what a physicist *does* when he measures 'space' and 'time' and to abandon, perhaps unconsciously, the 'is' of identity." (Korzybski, *op. cit.,* p. 648.)

My restricted use of the term *science* in this section has been made the object of attack on the ground that "all science is a search for truth." The implied *non sequitur* is that therefore all search for truth is science. I have elsewhere fully recognized the value of prescientific, nonscientific, and nonquantitative technics. (See G. A. Lundberg, "Is Sociology too Scientific?" *Sociologus,* IX, Sept., 1933, pp. 301, 302, 316-317. Also Ch. 3, note 11 below.) I use the term *science* to describe a method and its results, not to exalt that method or depreciate others. Also, I am dealing here only with the type of response known as generalization, i.e., the assumption of the general validity of propositions drawn from less than all the relevant data. Such assumptions may be made from single cases, but if so there is no basis upon which to estimate the probable validity of assumption.

21. W. Waller, "Insight and Scientific Method," *Amer. Jour. of Sociol.,* XL, Nov., 1934, p. 287. I refer to this article chiefly because it furnishes illustrations of the points I wish to make. It should not be inferred, therefore, that this author is especially hostile to quantitative methods. Since much of the controversial literature in sociology consists of heroic demolitions of positions nobody holds or defends, I cite in each case proponents of the views I attack. (For other illustrations see: A. Goldenweiser, "The Concept of Causality in the Physical and Social Sciences," *Amer. Sociol. Rev.,* III, Oct., 1938, pp. 626 ff.; J. F. Brown, "Towards a Theory of Social Dynamics," *Jour. Soc. Psych.,* VI, 1935, pp. 188-189; and K. Lewin, *A Dynamic Theory of Personality,* McGraw-Hill, 1935, pp. 12, 14, 31.)

22. J. F. Brown, "A Methodological Consideration of the Problem of Psychometrics," *Erkenntnis,* IV, 1934, pp. 46-61. Also his *Psychology and the Social Order,* McGraw-Hill, 1936, p. 32.

23. W. Waller, *op. cit.,* p. 288.

24. *Ibid.,* pp. 287, 288. My criticism of the use of "insight" and "understanding" as mysterious "methods" not subject of further analysis also applies to "creativeness," "genius," and "inspiration" as used for example in the following passage:

"The decadent periods, whether in art or science or religion, have *often been marked by this substitution of technique for genius; of specific training in technical skill* rather than real creativeness or inspiration. *In such periods, technique usually dominates the field;* scientists talk mainly of scientific technique with which they usually do not produce anything but mediocrity." (P. A. Sorokin, *Social and Cultural Dynamics,* I, American Book Co., 1937, p. 584.)

Exactly the opposite seems to me to be the fact. The close relationship between new technical departures and inventions on the one hand and epochs of scientific advance on the other seems to me to be about the most obvious fact which the history of science demonstrates. Indeed, how could it be otherwise if we regard science itself as a technic of achieving reliable knowledge? The close interdependence of the development of mathematics and other technical innovations and the most "creative" and "inspired" products of "genius" since the time of Newton, at least, is surely too well known to require even mention. One may disapprove, if one chooses, of the uses to which the technics that constitute science have been put. But these technics are none the less the *sine qua non* of scientific advance of every kind including that mysteriously called "inspirational creativeness." (See any history of science. For special aspects see William Harkness, "The Progress of Science as Exemplified in the Art of Weighing and Measuring," Annual Report of the Board of Regents of the Smithsonian Institution 1888, Government Printing Office, pp. 597-633. H. D. Hubbard, "The Romance of Measurement," *Scientific Monthly,* XXXIII, Oct., 1931, pp. 556-558.)

25. Waller, *op. cit.,* p. 290.

26. W. Köhler, *Gestalt Psychology,* Liveright, 1929, p. 361. Waller takes a similar position, *op. cit.,* pp. 285-290. Regarding the notion of "immediate experience" see E. C. Tolman, "Psychology versus Immediate Experience," *Philosophy of Science,* II, July, 1935, pp. 356-380.

27. See J. F. Brown, *The Mathematical Conceptions Underlying the Theory of Psychological and Social Fields,* Ann Arbor, Edwards Bros., Inc., 1935.

28. K. Koffka, *Principles of Gestalt Psychology,* Harcourt, 1935. In a footnote Koffka attributes a similar idea to Wertheimer. This is, of course, also the position of the present volume. We regard quantitative statements as merely *stated amounts* of qualitative attributes. That is, we regard all qualities as subject to distribution on a continuum in terms of the relative *amounts* of such quality. Under this interpretation, qualitative as well as quantitative aspects may be symbolically represented and manipulated mathematically.

29. Brown, *op. cit.,* p. 4.

30. Waller, *op. cit.,* p. 287.

31. N. Bohr, *Atomic Theory and the Description of Nature*, Macmillan, 1934, Ch. 4, pp. 106, 109, 110.

32. L. Bertalanffy, "Über die Bedeutungen der Umwälzungen in der Physik für die Biologie," *Biologisches Zentralblatt*, XLVII, 1927, pp. 653-662. See also on this subject Hans Müller, *et al.*, *Cold Spring Harbor Symposia on Quantitative Biology*, II, Biological Laboratory, Cold Spring Harbor, N.Y., 1934.

33. P. W. Bridgman, *The Logic of Modern Physics*, Macmillan, 1932, p. 37. "I believe that examination will show that the essence of an explanation consists in reducing a situation to elements with which we are so familiar that we accept them as a matter of course so that our curiosity rests. Reducing a situation to elements means, from the operational point of view, discovering familiar correlations between them."

34. W. Heisenberg, *The Physical Principles of the Quantum Theory*, University of Chicago Press, 1930, Ch. 4, pp. 58-59, 63.

35. S. Hecht, "The Uncertainty Principle and Human Behavior," *Harper's Magazine*, CLXX, Jan., 1935, pp. 237-249.

36. E. Schroedinger, *Science and the Human Temperament*, Norton, 1935, Chs. 2, 3, and 5, especially pp. 59, 64, 66, 131-132.

37. B. Russell, *The Analysis of Matter*, Harcourt, 1927, Chs. 16, 20, 30, 31, 35, 38. J. Dewey, *The Quest for Certainty*, Allen and Unwin, 1930, pp. 28, 191-192, 194, 198, 276. Also his *Logic. The Theory of Inquiry*, Holt, 1938, Ch. 22. For a more recent summary of the whole subject of quantification in science, see Harry Woolf, editor, *Quantification: A History of the Meaning of Measurement in the Natural and Social Sciences*, Bobbs-Merrill Co., 1961.

38. See L. K. Frank, "Causation: An Episode in the History of Thought," *The Journal of Philosophy*, XXXI, Aug. 2, 1934, pp. 421-428.

39. Operationally speaking, cause is imputed to the independent variable or combination of variables when it shows a high probability-expectation in its concomitant variations with other factors or combinations of factors, still other supposedly relevant conditions held constant.

40. See E. E. Eubank, *The Concepts of Sociology*, Heath, 1931.

41. See A. Korzybski, *Science and Sanity*, Science Press, 1933. This difficulty has been attributed to the survival of the first of Aristotle's three laws of thought, namely, the law of identity.

42. E.g., R. M. MacIver, *Society: Its Structure and Changes*, Long and Smith, 1931, p. 45. "They seek to apply mechanical methods of measurement to *things whose very nature* they fail to understand." [Italics mine.]

43. Cf. Carnap, *op. cit.*, pp. 29 ff.

44. See the articles by Walter Lippmann in the *New Republic*, XXXII, 1922, pp. 246-248, 275-277; XXXIII, 1923, pp. 145-146.

45. For recent illustration from two separate authors, see *Amer. Sociol.*

Rev., I, Feb., 1936, pp. 55, 75, 78. We have here another illustration of the tendency which I have discussed earlier in the present chapter to mistake the degree of formality of a process for fundamental difference in kind. Thus, the process of defining, especially when numbers are not employed, is not considered a form of measurement. Now, of course, for some purposes it may be useful to distinguish processes purely on the basis of the formality with which they are carried out. But in the present case where the issue involved is whether measurability is a trait, property, or characteristic inherent in phenomena or merely a rather formal and standardized way of responding, the essential operational identification of definition and measurement is of basic theoretic importance. Consider the following concession by Nagel: "Measurement has been defined as the correlation with numbers of entities which are not numbers. . . . But in a larger sense, in a sense to include most of those acts of identification, delineation, comparison, present in everyday thought and practice, numerical measurement is only infrequently used. . . . From this larger point of view, measurement can be regarded as the delimitation and fixation of our ideas of things so that the determination of what is to be a man or a circle is a case of measurement. The problems of measurement merge at one end with the problems of predication." (Ernest Nagel, "Measurement," *Erkenntnis,* II, 1931, p. 313.) Cf. John Dewey, *op. cit.,* p. 202: "What is here significant is that all comparison is of the nature of *measurement.* . . . The only difficulty standing in the way of recognition of the equipollence of comparison and measurement is the fact that the results of many measurements are stated qualitatively, not in numerical terms."

46. W. Waller, *Amer. Sociol. Rev.,* I, Feb., 1936, p. 59.

47. For some suggestions of this character, see A. F. Bentley, *Behavior Knowledge Fact,* Principia Press, 1935, Pt. III.

48. The theory and technique of sociological scale construction was greatly advanced by the wartime assignment of S. A. Stouffer, Paul Lazarsfeld, Louis Guttman, and their associates at the research branch of the Information and Education Division of the War Department during World War II. Their work revolutionized in many ways both the theory and practice of scale construction, application, and interpretation, and set forward by several decades the development of quantitative methods in sociology. The details of this development are reported in the fourth volume of *The American Soldier.* This monumental work and a subsequent enormous literature from 1950 down to the present time has rendered obsolete much argument on the subject that flourished before the Second World War.

Instead, the discussion has shifted to new and exciting vistas of further advance. Today many sociologists are occupied with mathematical models and refined experimentation, which seem to me to promise quiet but conclusive answers to the hoary obstacles that every generation has urged against the possibility of a science of sociology comparable with the well-recognized sciences. "Information Theory," "Cybernetics," "Game Theory," and other developments, together with the tremendous development of computational machinery in the last decade, definitely make possible today the orderly symbolic handling of data of a degree of complexity that has hitherto staggered the imagination of men generally and inhibited even the most venturesome and optimistic sociologists. Sociologists are beginning to realize that improved symbolic instruments and tools may be as important in unscrambling human relations as are electron microscopes and cyclotrons in physics.

49. Cf. H. Alpert, "Operational Definitions in Sociology," *Amer. Sociol. Rev.*, III, Dec., 1938, pp. 855-861.

50. Attention should here be called to the present connotations of such words as "attitude," "aptitude," and "skill." As generally used today throughout sociology and psychology they denote hidden, mysterious, and intangible entities rather than observable behavior. This is, of course, another illustration of the tendency to reify words and confuse them with the entities for which they are supposed to stand. Thus behavior of a certain kind is spoken of as *evidence of* intelligence of a certain kind or degree, the implication being that the behavior is merely a *sign* of the article itself. The thing itself turns out to be not further definable. It is a Kantian *ding an sich* or a Platonic "essence." It represents a metaphysical position which is incompatible with the metaphysics of modern science.

51. Nagel, *op. cit.*, p. 320. The basic issue involved in this position is the philosophical dichotomy between intensive and extensive qualities. It may be said at the outset that if one chooses to postulate such a dichotomy as inherent in phenomena, the reasoning leading to the conclusion here under attack regarding the immeasurability, or different logical nature of measurement, in the cases of certain phenomena doubtless follows. But I reject this postulate and accept instead the position of Bertrand Russell (*Principles of Mathematics,* Chs. 6, 69, pp. 164 ff.) and others which regards the extension-intension controversy as a purely conventional dichotomy like all other linguistic and logical constructs and, therefore, subject to modification whenever a modification promises a more adequate approach to the problems involved. Carnap's position regarding the proper function of logic is also relevant in this connection. (The above reference to Russell should not be taken to mean that my position on other matters is necessarily in accord with this work.)

52. Nagel (*op. cit.*, pp. 316-317) makes the excellent point that "it is important to remember, however, that the experimenter, working with marked or calibrated instruments, assumes that the calibrations indicate various qualitative continuities not *explicitly* present. The process of meas-

urement has not been fully exhibited until all those operations of calibration have been noted. When a weight is attached to a spring balance, and the position of a marker on the scale read, only a very small fraction of the process actually necessary to estimate the weight as five pounds has been observed; the operations entering into the construction and *correlation* of scale and spring must be included. It is of the essence of an experiment that it be repeatable. Therefore it is not the particular instrument used any more than it is the unique experiment which has such overwhelming importance in science; it is rather the repeatable process capable of producing the markings on the instrument which is. Every marked instrument implies the construction and existence of some standard series of *magnitudes* [italics mine], correlation with which constitutes the calibration. A wholehearted recognition of this reference of instruments to something beyond themselves, is a recognition that other characters of existence besides the spatial are capable of, and are involved in, the process of measurement."

53. For example, C. Kirkpatrick, "Assumptions and Methods in Attitude Measurement," *Amer. Sociol. Rev.*, I, Feb., 1936, pp. 75-88, says: "Counting people is measuring population directly by deriving multiples of units which are themselves part of the thing measured." (P. 80.) *Units* are *never* part of the "thing" measured. Units are symbols of human response. What is counted are symbolized responses to population. To count cells, families, weights, intelligence units, degrees of radicalism, etc., is to make different types of responses to population. But populations can be "measured" in all these respects by counting units appropriate to the type of response involved.

54. For a brilliant chapter on the meaning of "abstraction" and related subjects see A. F. Bentley, *op. cit.*, Ch. 21, "The Visibility of the Social," especially pp. 209-210. See also his Ch. 14 on "Isolationality."

55. In a more recent publication, "The Logic of Reduction in the Sciences," *Erkenntnis,* V, Aug.-Sept., 1935, pp. 46-51, Nagel takes a position quite compatible with that of the present chapter, although it does not deal with the specific problems here at issue. His emphasis upon the selectivity (abstractness) of all responses and, by implication, of all units and terms, may be a necessary elaboration, if not a contradiction, of his earlier view.

56. I am unconvinced by Nagel's criticism of Russell's position with respect to magnitude, namely, that the latter holds magnitude to be not "the ordered relations of and between existences, but as a domain of immaterial entities having no necessary reference to existence." (Nagel, *op. cit.*, p. 323.) Whatever may be the position of Russell in the work cited, I hold that the so-called "immaterial entities," namely, magnitudes, are *responses to something.* It is these responses, symbolically represented, which are subject to the manipulations constituting measurement. We may

extrapolate these responses into the "external" world and infer objects, qualities, or other "material" or "real" "things." All the so-called "concrete" actualities are inferred in this way. The mysterious words that lend a certain plausibility to Nagel's criticism above are "existence" and "common essences." Magnitudes, he apparently feels, are not "common essences" whereas pounds (?) are. These terms imply a postulate going beyond that to which science must confine itself, namely, that the only immediate subject matter with which science can deal is human responses.

I find Russell's position, even as set forth briefly by Nagel, correspondingly tenable: actual foot rules are *quantity*, their lengths are *magnitude*. It is only by an ellipsis that two quantities can be said to be equal; they are equal because they possess the same magnitude; and it is improper to say that one of two quantities is greater than the other; what is meant is that the magnitude which the first quantity possesses is greater than that of the second. (*Principles of Mathematics*, pp. 164 ff. Cited by Nagel, *op. cit.*, p. 324.)

Cf. also John Dewey, *op. cit.*, Ch. 11, especially p. 215: "When we apply the word *measure* to pounds, gallons, yards, etc., 'measure' is an elliptic expression for *means of measuring*." For a recent illustration of the confusion here under discussion see Mark May, "Ten Tests of Measurement," (*Educational Record*, April, 1939, pp. 200-220). "If two equal units of water, each having a density of 1, are poured together, the density of the resulting body is still 1." (P. 214.) Obviously, two *quantities* of water, the units of *volume* (magnitude) of which are added, cannot be expected to yield an additive result in units of *density*. Only the addition of *density* units could possibly yield such a result. See also Ch. VIII, Unabridged Edition, note 30.

57. C. Kirkpatrick, *op. cit.*, p. 80.

58. See Bentley's revealing analysis of the persistence of the assumption of the "basic," "natural" "existence" of the "individual person," "each assumed to have definite independent 'existence' and isolation, each in his own *locus* apart from every other. Here is direct descent in the mind-language from ancient 'souls,' each alone, face to face with its God." (*Op. cit.*, p. 29.) (See also his Ch. 14 on "Isolationality.") Bentley has also made concrete suggestions as to the type of units that may be basic to sociology. (*Op. cit.*, Chs. 23-25.) I believe that Michael and Adler (*Crime, Law, and Social Science*, Harcourt, 1932, pp. 82, 83) had a somewhat similar idea in mind when they declared that the social environment of man, *not* human behavior, is the proper subject matter of sociology. If so, I think their position is sound but badly stated and subject to misinterpretation. *Environment* cannot be either defined or studied except in terms of *behavior* with reference to some constant. The behavior of the constant is an implicit part of the situation. This is recognized in

the illustrations subsequently used by these authors. (*Ibid.*, pp. 84, 85.)

59. Kirkpatrick, *op. cit.*, p. 80. As for the contention that some measures are only indexes of that which is to be measured, this is merely to point out that in cases where we have previously established a correlation between two variables we sometimes find it more convenient to measure the one indirectly through the other. But this process is as practicable with reference to one type of units or phenomena as with another. Any measure of anything can be used as an index of any other measure of any other phenomenon, if the correlation between the two (which has to be first determined in any case) is reasonably constant.

60. *Ibid.*, p. 83.

61. *Ibid.*, p. 82.

62. *Ibid.*, p. 84.

63. It is even questionable whether cultural influences were less important in influencing this calibration than they are in calibrating societal measuring scales. The units of the metric system have nothing in common with units of the English measure. It is probable that present reactions to social phenomena vary from culture to culture more than do reactions to physical phenomena. The reason, however, is that physical science is already an international culture. In pre-scientific days the physical orientations of different tribes were perhaps no more uniform than their social.

64. Kirkpatrick, *op. cit.*, p. 84.

65. For the full details of how scale values are assigned to different statements, see L. L. Thurstone, "Attitudes Can Be Measured," *Amer. Journ. of Sociology*, XXXIII, Jan., 1928, pp. 529-554.

66. In using this illustration I am not here expressing any opinion as to the sociological value of attitude measurement, the validity or relative value of different types of scales, or other methods now employed or any of the other technical points involved. I have confined myself here solely to the *logical validity* of such measurement as a means of describing societal behavior and its logical comparability with other recognized measurement technics.

67. From the technological viewpoint, the most promising beginning along the line here indicated is in my opinion to be found in the work of S. C. Dodd, *A Controlled Experiment in Rural Hygiene in Syria*, Beirut University, and The Oxford Press, 1934, Pt. IV. Also his "A Theory for the Measurement of Some Social Forces," *Scientific Monthly*, XLIII, July, 1936. See also Read Bain, "Die Behavioristische Einstellung in der Sociologie," *Sociologus*, IX, March, 1933, pp. 28-44. For the most comprehensive theoretical outline on a mathematical level, see N. Rashevsky, "Outline of a Mathematical Theory of Human Relations," *Phil. of Sci.*, II, Oct., 1935. An able attempt at systematic sociological theory is L. von Wiese, *System der Allgemeine Soziologie*, 2nd ed., or L. von Wiese and

H. Becker, *Systematic Sociology*, Wiley, 1932. For valuable suggestions see also A. F. Bentley, *op. cit.*, and "Sociology and Mathematics," *Sociol. Rev.*, XXXIII, Oct., 1931; F. S. Chapin, *Contemporary American Institutions*, Harper, 1935, Pt. 5; J. F. Brown, "Towards a Theory of Social Dynamics," *Journ. Soc. Psych.*, VI, 1935, pp. 182-213; R. Mukerjee, "The Regional Balance of Man," *Amer. Journ. of Sociology*, XXXVI, Nov., 1930, pp. 455-460. The ecological approach is especially promising.

68. A recognition of the need of this step is found in the work of a special committee of the Social Science Research Council to define the term "acculturation" and to suggest more systematic research regarding the phenomenon. (See *Amer. Journ. of Sociology*, XLI, Nov., 1935, pp. 366-370. See also D. Young, *Amer. Journ. of Sociology*, XLII, July, 1936, pp. 95-99. See also C. W. Morris "Foundation of the Theory of Signs," *International Encyclopedia of Unified Science*, I, University of Chicago Press, 1938.) "But even without detailed documentation it has become clear to many persons today that man—including scientific man—must free himself from the web of words which he has spun and that language—including scientific language—is greatly in need of purification, simplification, and systematization. The theory of signs is a useful instrument for such debabelization." C. W. Morris, *op. cit.*, p. 3.

69. C. L. Hull, "The Conflicting Psychologies of Learning—A Way Out," *Psychological Review*, XLII, Nov., 1935, pp. 512-513.

70. F. Bacon, *Novum Organum* (tr. by J. Spedding), *The Works of Francis Bacon*, VIII, Taggart and Thompson, Boston, 1863, p. 78.

71. W. I. Thomas, *Primitive Behavior*, McGraw-Hill, 1937, p. 68.

72. See S. C. Dodd, *Dimensions of Society*, Macmillan, 1940.

73. *Ibid.*

74. See Read Bain, "Our Schizoid Culture," *Sociol. and Soc. Res.*, XIX, Jan.-Feb., 1935, pp. 266-276.

Chapter III

FRAMES OF REFERENCE IN SOCIOLOGY

A. The Nature of Selective Responses

MAN'S SENSORY EQUIPMENT does not permit him to study the whole universe in all its aspects at once. Hence his method of attack has always been to abstract out a segment or an aspect of the known universe in order to facilitate his study of it. The basis of abstracting a given field, or segmenting a total universe is, as we have seen, the nature of the problem or interest that actuates us. We respond to a tree, a forest, or to a whole landscape including both the tree and the forest according to the relationship in which we happen to find ourselves with respect to these objects. That is, our focus of attention is determined by the adjustment which the situation requires. This selective response we call our definition of the situation.

This definition, itself determined by the tensions (adjustment needs) of the organism, in turn determines the categories in terms of which we report our experience. The focus of a camera will likewise determine whether a tree, a forest, or a landscape is photographed. The fact that the last term includes the other two makes it neither a more nor a less useful "real," "existent," or "whole" category than the other two. We pointed out in the preceding chapters that all classifications, categories, or other terms designating objects or behaviors are of this character. The verbal delimitations of the universe which we make to correspond to these selective responses should be thought of, therefore, not as walls of separation, but rather as convenient ways of dealing with the situations that confront us.[1]

We may select aspects of a universe on geographic, historical, biological, or psychological, or any other basis which serves to frame our problems. Thus, naturalists find it convenient to define some universes geographically, both horizontally and vertically, into *regions* and to regard each as a field within which all of the interrelationships relevant to given problems are depicted. The ecologists' accounts of interdependence of life within each of these areas, horizontally defined, i.e., between geographic regions, are perhaps the best known. Vertically, naturalists also find it convenient to describe distinct strata from the ocean floor or under, to the stratosphere and beyond.[2] Biologists, psychologists, and sociologists frequently abstract fields on the basis of racial-cultural characteristics of the population—language, occupation, technological development—with or without reference to geographic location. The segregation of a field is always with reference to a problem on the part of the investigator rather than on the basis of assumed "natural" fields of data given in the universe itself.

Fields of study cannot be delimitated in terms of *kinds of matter* as is sometimes absurdly attempted. For example, it is sometimes carelessly stated that man is the "social unit" or the special concern of the social sciences, while metals and gases are the special concern of physics and chemistry. But obviously man may be just as legitimate a study for physics and chemistry as for sociology, depending on what aspect of his behavior, i.e., what problem we are interested in. Metals and gases may just as truly come within the purview of sociology for the same reasons, as a glance at monetary treatises or discussions of modern warfare will readily show. Every sample of interhuman behavior may be analyzed physically, chemically, biologically, physiologically, and sociologically.[3] In the same way a field of force as a frame of reference in science is *an abstraction of relevant behavior phenomena, symbolically represented,* which enables us to deal with one problem or set of problems at a time.[4]

B. *Frames of Reference*[5]

HAVING SELECTED FOR STUDY a problem or a set of related problems —an aspect of the universe—we seek to associate these data with what we already know, i.e., incorporate them into our already established habit-systems of response. When the new data or systems are so incorporated our intellectual tensions are released, our curiosity comes temporarily to rest, and we consider the new phenomenon "explained." When new observations are thus related to established associations and habits of thought, these new observations are declared to have "meaning," to be "understood," etc. Our already established habit-systems constitute what is usually called our frames of reference. We come by them as we come by any habits or habit-systems, namely, from the conditionings of all our environments, mainly, the social environment in the case of man. Usually man has a variety of these habit-systems, as a result of the necessarily selective nature of his responses, discussed above. Thus, he will have one habit-system of behavior (including thought) for members of his own tribe, another for all outside groups; one habit-system or frame of reference to which all *human* behavior is referred, another for all other animal behavior, as, for example, in pre-Darwinian days and to a large extent in present-day sociology. With widening experience, it frequently happens that two or more frames of reference which seemed originally mutually exclusive are found to overlap to a considerable degree. That is, it becomes doubtful as to which frame, or system, most adequately fits the phenomenon.[6] This means that the phenomenon may be associated with either habit-system in a way that is felt to be meaningful. On the other hand, the two interpretations may be conflicting and contradictory and, therefore, disturbing and destructive of that integrity, consistency, and balance toward which the organism tends.

The resolution of this tension or imbalance usually consists of the adoption of the framework which encompasses with the least resistance the largest variety of phenomena. This continuous integration of habits and habit-systems constitutes the growth and integration of personality. From this basic tendency of the organism toward equilibrium (i.e., toward its most probable state) is derived the principle of parsimony in science, as well as the search for simple unifying principles, gods, or demons, in all thought-systems. Accordingly, the tendency toward equilibrium involves the development of increasingly comprehensive frames of reference for the accommodation of increasing varieties of stimulations if, as is usually the case, the experiences of the organism throughout life continue to expand.

Categories, words, and symbols of every kind are, as we pointed out in the preceding chapter, designations of selective responses. Frames of reference (ideologies, theories, etc.) are systems of such words representing habits of responding with relative consistency to varieties of individual stimuli. As Thomas has pointed out, these responses must be interpreted in terms of the organism's definition of the situation.[7] This interpretation will in turn be determined by the situation and the pre-existing habit-systems. Every person necessarily functions according to *some* such habit-system or frame of reference unless he has a completely unintegrated or disorganized personality. These habit-systems are in folk language variously called "beliefs," "principles," or "philosophy of life."

C. *Classification of the Sciences*

IF IT IS agreed that all categories and classifications consist of symbolized selective responses determined by the nature of the problems (tensions) of the organism in a given situation, then the conventional classification of the sciences is also of this character. Delimitation of fields of knowledge has, of course, the same history and practical justification as selective responses of any other kind. That is, man's sensory equipment does not permit him to respond to the whole universe at once. Classifications being of the nature noted above, it follows that they may be expected to change—disintegrate or grow—from time to time. This has, of course, been true of classifications of the sciences. Since Comte first included sociology in a hierarchy of sciences about a hundred years ago, numerous other classifications have been made, and considerable argument has ensued as to the "correctness" of various classifications. Many of these discussions have been mainly a battle for prestige, the older and more conventionally recognized fields taking a patronizing attitude towards more recent branches of their own traditional domain, which break off and attain an independent status. Frequently, this independent status consists of little more than a separate administrative organization in the universities. Actually, of course, the only significant basis for the classification of the sciences is the problems to which each devotes itself. Since some problems are much more closely related than others in respect to the subject matter involved, degree of development, and equipment needed for their study, groupings of the sciences on this

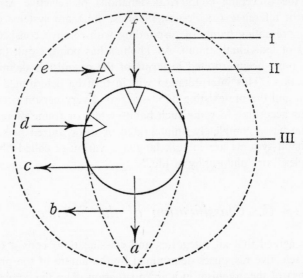

Fig. 1. The Field of the Sciences.   I, the domain of Things, the Cosmosphere. II, the realm of Organisms, the Biosphere. III, the kingdom of Man, the Sociosphere. The arrows indicate influences: (*a*) from III on II; (*b*) from II on I; (*c*) from III on I; (*d*) from I on III; (*e*) from I on II; (*f*) from II on III. (From Thomson and Geddes.)

basis will doubtless always be a convenience. It must always be kept in mind, however, that, as we have repeatedly emphasized above, these divisions should not be regarded as walls of separation in any way indicating a discontinuity of the universe, but merely as convenient devices for orderly division of labor.

From the above viewpoint as to the nature of classification it follows that an unlimited number of different classifications of the sciences might be made, each equally legitimate for any particular purpose that might interest the classifier. For the same reason, we must reject all attempts to make out that any given classification is inherent in nature or is intrinsically determined by the inherent "nature" of the subject matter. We take, on the contrary, the position that classifications of any kind are determined by the reactions of particular organisms, including all their conditionings, to those aspects of their situation which call for adjustment.

Accordingly, Comte's classification of the sciences in a hierarchy of mathematics, astronomy, physics, chemistry, biology, and sociology was doubtless suited to his own purposes and *as such* we have no objection to it. But his claim that each succeeding stage in the hierarchy depended upon those preceding it for its positive content, and his assumption that his hierarchy necessarily represents a trend of decreasing generality and increasing complexity is, of course, quite incompatible with the point of view here adopted.[8] A more tenable and useful view is to regard the sciences as having developed simultaneously and through interaction with each other, rather than serially in a one-way dependence. As for generality and complexity, the first chapter has already pointed out at some length that these are not inherent characteristics of phenomena but words describing man's response attitudes or manners, and as such entirely relative to the conditionings of the responder.

Much more suitable from our point of view is the preceding diagrammatic representation of the general field of the sciences by Thomson and Geddes [9] (Fig. 1, page 102).

A more detailed outline of the field of the sciences and one which is in every way compatible with our viewpoint is that represented in the accompanying chart from Malisoff. It not only shows the interrelationship and overlapping of the well-established sciences of today but includes the important feature of indicating probable future developments. This chart is an admirable summary of a subject which has received a great deal of incoherent discussion.[10]

Turning now to the more specific delimitation of the field of sociology, the accompanying chart from Sorokin is a good representation of our view. I am in full accord with the following extract from Sorokin's text accompanying this diagram:

"Sociology is interested only in those aspects of social phenomena and their relationships which are repeated either in time or in space or in both; which consequently exhibit some uniformity or constancy or typicality. Historical sciences paint the individual picture of the unique phenomenon studied (a certain person, institution, social object, social constellation of certain conditions); sociology gives either

an abstract formula (law) which describes (quantitatively or otherwise) a repeated uniformity (or the degree of variability) in the relationship between two or more societal variables, or a *type* as a composite photograph of the repeated social phenomena of a certain

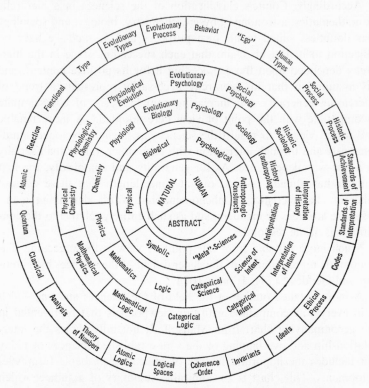

FIG. 2. An Arrangement of the Sciences.   (From Malisoff.)

kind. This difference sharply differentiates sociology from all historical disciplines.

"When this cardinal point is well understood, the nature of general as well as special sociologies becomes easily comprehensible. Under these conditions the task of *general* sociology may consist evidently in nothing but a study of those traits and relationships which are *common to all social phenomena*. To be common to all social phenomena means to be given in any social phenomenon wherever and whenever it exists or to be repeated any time and anywhere,

where any social phenomenon is given. *Through this subject-matter general sociology radically differs from all the other social sciences.* None of them studies this problem and none is competent to study it, as long as it remains a special social science. Each of these other

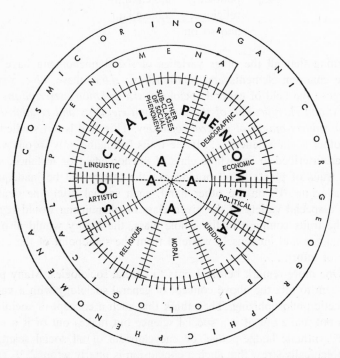

FIG. 3. The Relationship of the Sciences. (A) is the field of general sociology. The areas indicated by cross-hatched lines show the "interstitial" fields of special sociologies. The division of the whole field of social phenomena into a number of fields of social sciences is only illustrative.   (From Sorokin.)

social disciplines studies only its special variety of social phenomena: economics, the economic variety; political science, the political variety, and so on. But insofar as all these varieties are sub-classes of the same general class of social phenomena, they all must have, side by side with their specific characteristics and relationships, some traits and relationships common to all of them; otherwise they cannot belong to the general class of social phenomena and cannot be styled by a common name of the social sciences. Schematically this can be expressed in the following way. Let the following varieties of social phenomena consist of the following elements and relationships:

> economic: a,b,c,n,m,f,e
> political: a,b,c,h,d,j,p
> religious: a,b,c,g,i,q,r
> and so on

Granting that all the other varieties of social phenomena have the same common elements and relationships: *a,b,c,* these *a,b,c,* would compose the field of general sociology. *An isolation, description, analysis, and classification of these common elements and relationships is the subject-matter of general sociology.* This field is not studied by the other social sciences. . . . If the traits belonging only to one variety are ascribed to the whole class of phenomena (for instance, specific traits of plants to all organisms) the theory will be inadequate or fallacious. If, on the other hand, each special discipline dealing with a special variety of the given class of phenomena would repeat all the traits common to the whole class, the theory would also be inadequate and immensely wasteful from the standpoint of the economy of effort. . . .

"One more remark before I pass to special sociologies. Many people seem to mix the above concept of general sociology with a vague synthetic philosophizing. They think that such a concept of sociology does not make out of it a special science but makes out of it a kind of a 'synthetic hodge-podge' or encyclopedia of all social sciences. I emphatically stress that such a conclusion is utterly wrong." [11]

The characteristics and relationships common to all societal phenomena or social situations are, then, the proper concern of the field of general sociology. It still remains to designate more concretely all the varieties of such phenomena. After further consideration of this subject in a later chapter we shall conclude that interhuman activity (including intrahuman or "inner" behavior which has other people as a point of reference) constitutes the common element of all social situations and is, therefore, the principal general subject of our study. So far, this is merely a formal and tautological definition, for we have said that interhuman behavior is the common element in all social situations, and have then defined social situations as those in which interhuman behavior is present. This is, as we shall show in the next chapter, analogous to the procedure involved in the formal statement of the law of inertia in physics. The statement that if no force acts on a body in motion, it continues to move uniformly in a straight line, is logically and inevitably true if we define force as that which deflects a moving body from its uniform motion in a straight line. The *practical* and operational definition and significance of this law depends upon our ability to construct instruments for the reliable measurement of "force," "motion," and "straight line," in terms of which we can estimate the probability of a certain kind of motion in concrete, observable instances. In the same way, the above definition of social behavior as that in which interhuman activity is present gains practical scientific significance only when this activity is reduced to units in terms of which we can predict the probability of designated types of observable behavior *in concrete cases*. To call attention to this subject matter and to indicate the method by which such prediction can be made will be our principal concern. *To work out such predictions for all important types of social behavior* must be the main task of practical sociologists' research as long as man has problems of social adjustment to solve.

If we have succeeded in making clear that the symbols and symbolic systems (including science) with which man designates his reactions to phenomena are of the above nature, that is, merely convenient man-made maps or coordinates for the correlation of human experiences, an important object will have been achieved. For one thing, it will then be possible to avoid all arguments involving the absolutes of "truth," "falsity," or other metaphysical characterizations of the framework to be proposed. Also, it will be unnecessary to discuss all problems of whether the entities designated by our terms "exist" or not, for we have at the outset postulated the "existence" of that which precipitates the responses designated by the categories and symbols we have adopted. By the same reasoning it becomes unnecessary for us either to deny or to provide a place in our system for all the *words* that have ever been used by other students in other frameworks designating societal phenomena. We do obligate ourselves to provide a place in our system for all communicable observations of societal behavior. In short, we wish to change the level of sociological discussion, as has already been done in the other sciences, from its traditional plane of metaphysical name-calling to the plane of systematic determination of utility.

Do the coordinates (the meridians, parallels, pigeon-holes, map, or verbal framework) of our system provide a convenient set of reference points for the correlation of societal knowledge? Is it a framework which serves to a superior degree the requirements of comprehensiveness, parsimony, objectivity, and verifiability? Does the system offer opportunity for and the means of the extension, refinement, and verification of knowledge through systematic research? Does it promise the induction of laws from which reliable predictions of societal behavior may be made? These are the questions which have interested us in developing the viewpoint and the framework outlined below.

D. The Sources of Frames of Reference

WE HAVE ELABORATED above on the thesis that frames of reference, philosophies, or any other such systems whatsoever consist of symbolic behaviors representing the behaver's interpretation of the world in which he lives. As such, frames of reference have the same source as any other societal phenomena, namely, the more or less formally selected residue of the accumulated experience of the group. In a large society in which a high degree of division of labor exists various groups are likely to be exposed to differing environments and consequently develop differing frameworks to suit their differing experiences. A multitude of barriers, lack of communication, the phenomena of prestige, authority, vested interests, the inertia of habit, and institutionalization, usually operate to inhibit the facile adjustments of symbolic frameworks to changing experiences. At present we are interested only in pointing out that since frameworks of reference are not given in nature but are constructs of man's convenience, man will in the long run select or construct them from the sources and by the methods which his experience has shown to be most useful in the past.

If we survey the various frames of reference which have throughout history been invented and employed by man to order the phenomena of his world, we find a large and conglomerate variety, namely all the philosophies and ideologies of all peoples and ages. It happens that out of this variety there has emerged by a series of successive changes the framework of modern natural science, the nature of which we have elaborated in the first chapter. The growing dominance of this frame of reference, its viewpoint and method, may be deplored but it can hardly be denied. New problems and new fields will, whether we realize it or not, inevitably be approached by some method that has been found useful in other, however remotely similar, situations. We are, in fact, totally helpless in a new situation unless we can define it in terms of situations with which we are already familiar. Our method of approach must in any case, as already noted, be drawn from the accumulated experience of the ages. That is, if we do not "imitate" the framework and methods of natural science in seeking to further our knowledge of the societal universe, we shall (unless we rely on direct revelation) assuredly imitate the methods of theology, astrology, or some other system or combination of systems that has enjoyed great vogue in the history of mankind.

Under these circumstances it would be strange indeed if social scientists were not increasingly influenced by the theories and methods of modern science. In fact, the scientific explanation of any phenomenon usually consists of treating a new and hitherto unexplained phenomenon as a special illustration of an older or more familiar process, or law of behavior. If, therefore, we draw upon the present structure of natural science for suggestions for a framework within which sociological phenomena can be most conveniently comprehended, such action should hardly need either explanation or defense.

Nor should it be necessary to explain that this does not mean that we intend to "force" any sociological data into the units of any other science unless the latter serve the purposes of sociology. Every science adopts the categories and the units which best serve its own purposes, but no one has any difficulty in recognizing the common framework, the common rules of logic, and the common tests of validity of all the sciences. Neither does the use of the same mathematical symbols and operations in different sciences constitute "forcing" the data of one into the other any more than the use of the same nouns and verbs in physics and in poetry make these fields the same. No one proposes to put a specimen of society in a test tube for analysis or to measure sociological phenomena with the instruments of the physics laboratory. If we attempt to construct for the measurement of sociological phenomena instruments based on the same logical foundations as those of physics, that is an entirely different matter. This will become sufficiently clear as we proceed.

E. The Need and Requirements of Scientific Sociological Theory

EVERYONE PROBABLY AGREES that the backbone of any science is a series of relevant, verifiable, consistent generalizations called principles, or laws. It will probably be further agreed that to attain such a set of principles it is necessary first to formulate a set of hypotheses and second to test them empirically. Does sociology today have a frame of observation, description, and interpretation which can be employed by the great body of investigators in a concerted attack upon sociological problems?

For some years I have examined the annual grist of sociological researches as they are reported. In addition to my interest in the details of method I have had in mind such questions as the following: What hypothesis or theory does this research formulate or proceed upon? What generalization or principle of sociology is more firmly established or is rendered more dubious by the results of this research project? If all these studies had succeeded in achieving their alleged objective, would the verifiable sum total of scientific societal knowledge be increased noticeably? If ten thousand similar studies were made, would our framework of scientific principles be measurably stronger? I am forced to the conclusion that for most of the researches I have seen, the answer to each question would be of a negative character.

This does not mean that these researches have been useless. Frequently they have provided valuable material for public agitation, propaganda, and desirable social reforms. Many have definitely contributed to more intelligent administration of public affairs. All the studies have provided for the most part harmless employment and sometimes desirable training for the people engaged in them. Thus they have been instrumental in redistributing the wealth, which is generally regarded as desirable. The studies have frequently contributed to the entertainment and societal knowledge of the reading public. All of these results are entirely desirable or at least defensible, and so long as they do not demand to be taken more seriously, they should not be criticized for contributing little or nothing to the science of sociology. Nor is it my purpose to make derogatory comparisons between such types of research [12] and that directed avowedly at the advancement of science. But since the latter is generally conceded to be basic in the long run, it is permissible to inquire why so small and doubtful a portion of sociological research is fundamentally scientific.

The main reason appears to be that there exists for sociology no coherent body of scientific theory with reference to which research can be undertaken or evaluated. There is no workable set of postulates to guide and organize research. There is a vast amount of common-sense generalizations about alleged uniformities in social behavior. In the absence of anything more reliable, even these are useful. But they hardly conform to the requirements of scientific theory. In the first place, if the implicit assumptions underlying this lore are examined, it will be found to consist almost entirely of animistic, anthropomorphic, and theological postulates. This is to be expected since most of this folklore has come down to us from a time when these orientations dominated nearly all thinking. In the second place, both the theories and the generalizations of contemporary sociology are couched in terms which have never been objectively or operationally defined. They are, on the contrary, for the most part of a metaphysical character and not susceptible of empirical test. Finally, the existing theories and generalizations have never been satisfactorily systematized in terms and assumptions compatible with modern science as set forth above.

The need for such systematization has been recognized by all the leading thinkers and all of them have made brilliant attempts in this direction. The works of A. Comte, H. C. Carey, F. Le Play, H. Spencer, L. F. Ward, V. Pareto, and L. von Wiese are important illustrations of man's struggle toward more and more comprehensive frameworks for the correlation of his experiences. The development of new and more delicate instruments and technology of observation, notably in the "physical" sciences, has, it is true, rendered the systems of these men largely obsolete. Consider, for example, the effect upon these systems of the developments in physiological knowledge which forced the abandonment of the instinct hypothesis and the whole attendant super-structure of pre-behavioristic psychology. One of the most important by-products of the latter for sociology has been, as pointed out in preceding chapters, a new orientation regarding symbolic behavior and the nature of the processes conventionally included under terms like "mind" and "knowledge." The result has been a desperate attempt to piece together fragments of old sociological systems with the framework of modern science, the dominance of which can no longer be denied, ignored, or kept within a reservation mysteriously labeled "physical." The present system has been formulated largely as a result of this situation.

F. A Natural Science Theory of Human Society

1. THE FIELD-CONCEPT IN SCIENCE

In the present system we shall regard all societal phenomena from the dynamic point of view as interhuman behavior (including intrahuman behavior which has other people as a point of reference). This behavior we shall consider as subject to interpretation within the same framework as any other kind of behavior. That is, we shall regard it as *movement within a field of force in time*. Observable manifestations of behavior will be regarded as functions of *energy*, defined here as in other sciences, in terms of measurable amounts of change. The field [13] of force is here, as in other sciences, defined as that segment of the universe which for given purposes of study, with the sensory and symbolic apparatus we command at present, we find it convenient or relevant to define as the situation. The situation always consists of the responding entity and its total environment regarded as a closed system not influenced from the outside. The ultimate objective of science, *as science,* is to discover predictable sequences and correlations between the phenomena of the selected field.

The explanation of social groupings and their behavior as groups is generally regarded as the basic problem of sociology. Accordingly, any comprehensive social theory must provide a logically consistent description of this phenomenon. All systematic thinkers on the subject have recognized this need and they have, therefore, usually advanced some generalized principle, such as gregarious instincts, consciousness of kind, class consciousness, etc. The main difficulty with these theories has been that they have posited within the individual or the group some mechanism, itself unexplained or only implicitly accounted for, by which the observed behavior was to be explained. This approach is in striking contrast to that which physical science has found so useful, namely, that the behavior of any particle or aggregate is to be explained mainly in terms of the structure of the field within which it operates. The swing toward this position in sociology is evidenced by the increasing emphasis upon the situation (of which the individual or the group under consideration is always a part) rather than upon the individual characteristics of the behaving entity.[14]

Geographers and ecologists have given one type of recognition to the situational or field interpretation of social behavior. In fact, the ecologists' concept of a region is a special case of what is here meant by a field. *Region,* as the ecologists use the term, always involves geographic space.[15] The concept of *field* which is of such vast importance in physics also has this implication of geographic space. So thorough is our habituation to this use of the word "space" that we have reified it into an entity which, it is frequently assumed, can be legitimately used only in reference to certain geographic situations and that the use of spatial terms in discussing societal and psychological phenomena is merely figurative. We shall here take the position that all relational thinking tends to structure itself in spatial terms and that the notion of social and psychological space is as valid as the notion of geographic space. Space in mathematics (and in sociology) merely means a manifold (a number of entities related under one system) in which *positional relationships* of any kind may be expressed. The use of spatial constructs in sociological description is, of course, very common as, for example, when we speak of high and low status, social mobility, social boundaries, distance, and barriers.[16] This is as legitimate and useful employment of spatial concepts as is their use in geography, ecology, or physics. Let us review briefly the history of the gradual expansion of the use of spatial or field constructs in the description of societal relationships.

The geographers and ecologists at first emphasized the purely geographic, structural, and spatial relationships of the community. The mapping and charting of these features admittedly provided a useful framework within which to interpret many aspects of community behavior. Fortunately, the technic of symbolizing on paper such facts as area, direction, topography, channels of communication, land utilization, economic areas, etc., by maps and airplane photographs is widely accepted and understood. There are several reasons for the general understanding of this kind of symbolic representation. In the first place, in its most elementary forms it is a kind of picture-writing. Secondly, the cartographic and photographic types of representation have thus far been applied chiefly to those aspects of the community which are conspicuously incorporated in the so-called material culture, for the objective study of which our technics have always been more highly developed. As a result, we ascribe to those aspects of the community which can be depicted or represented by the simpler cartographic methods a "tangibility," "concreteness," and "reality" which we withhold from aspects for which we have not yet developed objective symbolic technics.[17]

The next step after mere mapping in the process of describing the community was to convert behavior itself into symbolic indexes which can in turn be represented in geometric, isometric, isotypical, or gradient terms.[18] Thus birth, death, disease, and delinquency rates or any other behavior phenomena can be computed for local areas and the relationship of such phenomena to these regions can be shown by lines representing gradients or other geometric devices. A line on the same map representing the declining delinquency rate from the center of the city toward the periphery, denotes a phenomenon just as actual, observable, and meaningful as a line representing the main street. Yet such is the degree of our unfamiliarity with such abstractions as rates, that we feel the line representing the street has a certain "reality," legitimacy, and relevance to the "true" representation of a community which it is felt the delinquency gradient has not. Both types of lines represent both a structural and a functional phenomenon. At present, many of these behavior phenomena have not yet been metricized. Until they are reduced to metric units we may deal with them by topological constructs, or in terms of symbolic logic, which may be an intermediate step toward metrical statement.[19] The correlation[20] of these various indexes when worked out for *all* the relevant aspects of community behavior would represent all the description and explanation of the life of a community which science can attain. For this description, multiplied and generalized, would say in a more precise and verifiable fashion all that is factually valid in all the wordy and obscure treatises we now have on the community.

The aspect of the community which this approach seems to neglect is the so-called "human" psychological factors of social interaction itself. Hence the next step is to invent objective devices for the representation of these processes which are at present dealt with largely in the language of literature and philosophy.

The transition in the technic of representation from an ecological spot or rate map of delinquency to the organization or functional chart represents merely a transition (1) from geographic to social space representation and (2) from the relatively pictorial technic of the delinquency map to a perhaps more abstract form of symbolic representation of the behavior depicted by the functional chart. That is, the lines in an organization chart do not correspond to roads, railways, etc., in geographic space but represent relationships in social space,[21] such as the relation of the major to subordinate officials, just as a political boundary or a delinquency gradient represents a behavior phenomenon relating two areas of a city in geographic space. In both cases the lines stand fundamentally for behavior phenomena, which are the concern of science. In the same way, purely topological representations or the characters of symbolic logic are merely other literary methods of representing relations. These points are made for the benefit of those who feel that any other language than the customary philosophical terminology of discussing the subtler community relations is "artificial," "cold," "rigid," and lacking in color. All symbolic representation of behavior is "artificial" in exactly the same way. The coldness, rigidity, and lack of color of the topological and mathematical symbolism may be the best reason for its superiority as scientific language. It is, in fact, because philosophical vocabulary is so suffused with subtle and varied emotional tones and meanings that it turns out to be largely useless in scientific discourse and tends to be supplanted by geometric and other mathematical symbols.[22] It is significant to note how well other sciences get along in explaining the most intricate phenomena without any of the type of language alleged to be so essential in sociology.

The basic assumption of ecologists and others who have attempted to chart the community is that the structures which they depict represent the channels of societal energy (the time-rate of societal change), or the static aspect of the type of behavior we call societal. This assumption also meets the common objection to the ecologists' technic, that it does not portray the dynamic interactions which are the essence of social activity. Just as the trend of development has been from mapping geographic features to the spatial representation of group behaviors of the more obvious (i.e., formally recorded) type, so the next step is to develop technics of representing in their significant relationships the subtler (i.e., as yet imperfectly understood) energy currents or forces that animate and define a community. These patterns are here regarded as existing in social space as well as in geographic space. It has become highly conventional and useful to represent the latter by charts, maps, and other geometric and mathematical devices. The adequate representation of relationships in social space may likewise be greatly facilitated by a kind of sociography, or sociological or cultural ecology.

In short, we use the term "field" in this book as equivalent to W. I Thomas' "situation," because we want to emphasize that the methods of "field" analysis developed in other sciences are also applicable to "situations." We frequently find it convenient to represent and talk about societal situations in spatial terms. The ecologist defines a *region* as any convenient geographic area within which interaction of its components, organic and inorganic, takes place. Our "field" is a more general construct in that it includes not only such geographic areas or regions but also purely sociological regions which may or may not have definite geographic boundaries. For example, the phenomena which constitute Catholicism and Communism (i.e., the behavior of Catholics and Communists) cannot be adequately bounded geographically but may be meaningfully discussed in social-spatial terms as mutually exclusive fields, at a maximum distance from each other, with mutually impermeable boundaries, and so on. Or the field may be defined as religion, which might include both of the above, the purpose being to study the relationship of the two. After the field has been selected the problem is to *structure* it somehow so that the relationship of the elements in the field can be most accurately shown. The method of doing this with which we are most familiar is, of course, to name with words certain elements or factors in the situation and then by use of the adjectives and verbs of ordinary language we attempt to give an accurate statement of the relationships within the field. If the field happens to be a simple organism, a picture of its anatomy may be referred to as a frame within which discussion of the relationship of various parts can conveniently be carried on. Frequently, however, the teacher finds that a schematic drawing of the anatomy or the nervous system is a more convenient device for throwing certain relationships into bold relief than is an actual animal or a picture of the animal. That is, an abstraction, leaving out all the details except those to which it is desired to call attention communicates the idea more readily. The more elementary diagrams confine themselves to showing relationships of position, symmetry, and size in nonmetrical terms. More refined analysis leads to gradients, potentials, and functional equations, the highest development of which involves metric units. Thus fields may be structured in varying degrees, from mere discussion in folk-terms, or simple diagrams showing, for example, one factor completely inclosed in another to a multi-dimensional system of mathematical coordinates.

Nearly everyone is accustomed to the simpler examples of the above method of analysis and takes its validity for granted. Yet a diagram of the anatomy of a starfish is a symbolic representation or abstraction of a behavior-complex—a situation, a field—just as truly as is a diagrammatic representation of the mutual exclusiveness or other relationships of the two behavior-complexes called Communism and Catholicism. Again, this degree of abstraction is fairly conventional and creates no great objection as a device for the representation of sociological phenomena. But if a grid representing mathematical coordinates is substituted for one of these schematic drawings (e.g., to represent quantitatively gradients or functional interdependence), many people whose symbolic equipment does not extend to this level, begin to feel worried. They feel that this is getting away from "reality," "leaving something out," "taking the life out of the situation," etc. Doubtless they are right if they mean by reality individual cases and concrete instances in *all* their relationships. Science aims at quite other goals, namely, *certain specified relationships* which are *generally true, within rigidly specified conditions*. The more advanced science becomes, the more abstract it becomes, and yet—the more powerful are the abstractions it evolves. As Einstein and Infeld have said: "The simpler and more fundamental our assumptions become, the more intricate is our mathematical tool of reasoning; the way from theory to observation becomes longer, more subtle, and more complicated. Although it sounds paradoxical, we could say: Modern physics is simpler than the old physics and seems, therefore, more difficult and intricate." [23] Although this process consists from one point of view of learning more and more about less and less, yet such is the general validity of the scientist's abstraction that the "less and less" which he abstracts is found practically applicable to more and more.[24]

Familiarity with the symbolism of mathematics and symbolic logic is, of course, growing rapidly and their more elementary applications to sociological phenomena are already common. For example, where *two* types of phenomena vary concurrently, it is quite customary, if they have been reduced to metric units, to plot them on a two-dimensional graph. Such a simple line graph is felt to be a more adequate representation of the co-variation of the two types of phenomena than a "literary" paragraph attempting to describe the fluctuations. Indeed, if the fluctuations are at all intricate they cannot be represented with any degree of adequacy except by the graphic technic. The relationship of the two phenomena may, of course, be further generalized and summarized in the form of a coefficient of correlation or a mathematical equation, which is the goal at which all scientific generalizations aim.

Now the two-dimensional system of coordinates upon which relationships are represented is already so conventional that even the report cards of elementary school children employ graphs to communicate to parents the quality of a child's work in different subjects in relation to the norm for different ages. But the limitations of a frame of reference which allows only two variables is apparent to everyone, and this limitation has doubtless contributed to the feeling that the method described above has little or no applicability to really involved sociological situations in which the number of factors reacting on each other may be very numerous. More elaborate technics of representation are unquestionably required for such situations and the future of sociology as a science depends on their development. The technics of multi-dimensional coordinates, matrix and factor analysis have been developed in response to precisely this need.[25] They and others yet to be invented promise to provide these more adequate structures of sociological fields which will make possible a more systematic and refined analysis of the relationships among the components of societal situations. The steps in the construction of a scientific system are the same in any field. Many thoughtful people, including scientists of distinction and unquestioned competence in their own fields, genuinely feel that there are certain differences between the subject matter of the physical and the social sciences which preclude the applicability of the same general methods to both. (See note 5.) Without contradicting the position of these men in what they have to say regarding the shortcomings of much work in all the sciences and especially in the social sciences, it seems to me to be an overstatement to say or to imply that there are *no* rules of logic as well as *no* rules of procedure that characterize distinctively the behavior of scientists as scientists. If by "scientific method" or "methods" is meant the concrete procedures and paraphernalia of the different sciences, there can be no question regarding the variety of scientific procedures. After all, microscopes are employed in some sciences and telescopes in others. But surely there are generally valid principles and *methods* of sampling, correlation, probability computation, and logical inference to which nearly all scientists subscribe. Surely every scientist has in mind *some criteria* on the basis of which he undertakes to characterize both his own work and that of others as "scientific" or nonscientific. *These criteria* are what I have in mind when I use the phrase "scientific method" in this book. A distinguished physiologist has described the procedure as follows: [26]

"The first step in building up the conceptual scheme of a new generalized system is the recognition, by induction, of a sufficiently definite class of phenomena like those classes designated by the terms dynamical system, physico-chemical system, and economic system. This is followed by the discrimination, definition, and choice of the abstract entities, like components, temperature, and pressure, that suffice for the characterization (to a certain approximation) of the system. This choice is limited by observation and experiment; it is determined by observation, experiment, logical and mathematical considerations, and by convenience. The closer the approximation that is sought, the greater, in general, will be the number of abstract entities that must be accounted for. Moreover, if the treatment is to be mathematical, it is necessary to set up mathematical functions or indices like concentrations in chemical equivalents per liter, temperature on the absolute scale, or pressure in atmospheres, corresponding to the chosen abstract entities. . . .

"The finding of the equations for the class of systems is the discovery of general laws (uniformities) that are descriptive of the class of systems, and the appropriate application of these laws in the form of equations. In the case of a particular concrete system, numerical values, for example, a particular mass, concentration, or temperature, or the numerical value of some other particular constant (parameter), have to be introduced. Such equations are commonly spoken of as the conditions. In the more advanced sciences the most general conditions are likely to be expressed in the form of differential equations.

"For the *complete* description of the conditions by means of equations, the results of counting or of measurement are indispensable. Therefore, it may be impossible to set up the equations. *But it is evident that this does not affect the logic.*" [Italics mine.]

It will be noticed that three major steps in the construction of a scientific system are specified above. First, there is the selection of a "definite class of phenomena." This we have done above in the quotation from Professor Sorokin. The second step is the "discrimination, definition and choice of the abstract entities, like components ... that suffice for the characterization (to a certain approximation) of the system." Finally, there is the generalization of the uniformities observed in the behavior of the components selected. We discussed in the preceding chapter the implications of this requirement as regards quantitative methods. But it is profitable also to describe hypothetically the relationships in nonmetrical mathematical symbols.

The limitations and necessarily tentative nature of the formulations possible in the present stage of sociological development must be clearly recognized. The history of the other sciences suggests the type of developments which we must expect in systems of sociology. But this is no reason for not attempting systematization. In the presence of highly developed systems there is a tendency to forget the long, painstaking, and undramatic labors of the thousands upon whose labors these systems rest. Social scientists are frequently staggered by the task which remains to be accomplished if their fields are to be brought up to a level of other sciences. As a result, they are inclined to regard their field as not amenable to such treatment. We are prone to remember only the dramatic high points in the history of science, which we like to ascribe to flashes of genius. The facts in the history of sciences as in all other examples of high achievement indicate instead a slow and laborious growth. Henderson has summarized the situation admirably when he says: [27]

"The present knowledge of organic chemistry is the accumulated result of countless experimental researches, the equivalent of the work of not less than two or three thousand intelligent and highly skilled specialists working with perfected methods for a lifetime. In the beginning the classification of organic compounds was very simple and inadequate. It is today perhaps the most complex and elaborate classification that exists, and it has reached this condition by a long process of evolution through adaptations to the facts. *Social scientists are prone to overlook such considerations. Yet, there is no reason to doubt that the necessary conditions for the development of any science that deals with complex material are similar. Among these conditions we may recognize (1) an immense amount of methodical, systematic, skilled labor and (2) the use of theories and classifications. The theories are at first crude and the classifications simple, but by adaptation to the facts the theories are refined and the classifications made complex.* . . . [Italics mine.]

"In order to make use of variables, definitions are necessary, and when the facts are very complex, classification is necessary for definition. Thus, where complex classification is necessary, some provisional classification must, in general, precede the use of mathematics, or even of the kind of logic that the experience of applied mathematics has taught. This is almost intuitively perceived by those who set to work seriously on the facts, but it is not so plain to the onlookers."

2. Requirements of a Natural Science Theory

Having chosen to regard interhuman behavior in its most generalized form as a system of energy operating within a field of force, we next postulate that similarities and differences of characteristics, behavior, intensity of interaction, attractions, and repulsions—imbalances of whatever sort—within this total system determine the direction and the vigor of the flow of this energy. The vigor and direction of the flow of this energy in turn determine the configurations, the structure, the sequences, and the correlations in the behavior of human groups. The similarities and the differences or imbalances which determine the flow of societal energy may be of any kind —social-spatial (status), temporal, (e.g., age), sexual, economic, esthetic, temperamental, developmental, ideational, or any other. Specific behavior of any kind is then regarded as the resultant of all these similarities and differences, attractions and repulsions, as they operate in the delimited field of force (the situation) within which any or all of the factors or components may influence any or all of the others. The central task of sociology is to formulate predictable sequences (principles) of behavior within situations so standardized and defined as to allow the use of these principles in *any* situation whose significant deviations from the standardized situation can be measured.

This last requirement raises several considerations of fundamental importance in science. First, as will be further elaborated in the next chapter, it emphasizes the *generality* or abstractness of scientific principles or laws. They rarely, if ever, describe actual occurrences in uncontrolled nature. They merely provide norms from which individual, actual occurrences can be predicted within measurable probability-expectations, because of the carefully defined (measured) conditions always attached to scientific laws describing the highly abstract and standardized circumstances under which the law holds. Except for this general standardized and abstract character of scientific laws, we should, of course, require a different law for each event in the universe. Secondly, the necessary generality of scientific laws requires that they be organized into a *system* compatible with each other and in terms of which all the behavior within the field can be described. That is, the system must be comprehensive. At the same time it should involve as few assumptions and basic terms as possible. Such systems afford a minimum of mental conflict and a maximum of convenience as an adjustment technic. Thirdly, a system is needed for the correlation of research so as to make it bear directly and with greatest economy of effort upon the problems (hypotheses) the field presents. Only within a carefully formulated system can cooperative effort as well as orderly verification or refutation take place.

A system requires, as we have said, that certain common factors or components of the selected universe, preferably few, be selected in terms of the variation of which all concrete situations can be described. This has been recognized by all systematizers and such "basic" factors are accordingly present in all systems. Spirits governing specific department of the universe were basic components of many early systems. In others, a single such spirit endowed with all necessary attributes, is found. In Newtonian physics such factors as mass, time, and space are used as basic factors in terms of which all of the phenomena of a certain aspect of the universe are comprehended. When we turn to the social sciences, we find a great variety of such basic factors proposed. The most popular and prevalent type of factorization among the systematizers of the recent past have been the systems of instincts,[28] interests, wishes, and "residues." In some of these cases the authors labored under the delusion that they were in pursuit of and had discovered "ultimate realities" of some sort instead of convenient hypotheses in terms of which societal behavior could be coherently described. That is, theirs was a thinly veiled search for the historic philosopher's stone which would unlock all the doors to all knowledge.

The increasing pervasiveness of the methods and results of the "physical" and biological sciences, notably the development of behavioristic psychology, has in recent decades rendered the above type of approach untenable and has led to a point of view closely related to and compatible with the system proposed in the present volume. Thus, Sumner and Keller [29] find in (1) man, and (2) land, two basic factors the ratio of which affords a point of reference for the explanation of much societal behavior. W. I. Thomas' [30] approach in terms of the interaction of *habit systems* (of human groups) to situations (total environment as defined, i.e., selectively responded to, by individuals or groups) represents a more dynamic and useful set of categories in that the emphasis is here on behavior-units.[31] Other scholars have adopted other concepts as basic to the system they espouse. From such attempts by many minds in different times and places there emerges gradually the more stable and verifiable conceptual schemes that constitute, at any given time, acceptable and accepted scientific theory.[32]

G. Conclusion

WE HAVE NOTED repeatedly in these introductory chapters, that man reacts selectively to the universe according to the condition of the organism in relation to the situation in which it finds itself at a given time. These selective responses when symbolized become the words, sentences, categories, classifications, and formulas with which we describe and explain our universe. They range from the symbols for an individual experience of the most isolated sort to the classification of the sciences and to theories of the most comprehensive scope. These symbolic frames of reference constitute habit-systems according to which we order our responses.

In the second place we noted that relational thinking tends to structure itself in spatial terms. We find it convenient to discuss segments of the universe within a frame conventionally called a "field" in some sciences and a "situation" in sociology. Thus the sociological field is a space within which, for convenience of study, we assemble all the phenomena relevant to the explanation of a specimen of societal behavior, regardless of the diffusion of these phenomena in geographic space. These sociological fields or situations, being themselves frames of reference, are delimited by the same process of selective responses, as mentioned above. A field or a situation is delimited by the adjustment-needs of the observer. That is, all behavior is relative to the behaver's definition of the situation. The symbols in terms of which he makes that definition and his reactions to the situation as defined in these symbols constitute the data for sociological study. It follows that the "field" as defined above then includes not only the geographical area and other people, but also all the symbols and symbolic behavior representing gods, demons, taboos, beliefs, and ideologies of everybody in the field.[33] The fact that these latter items can be observed or inferred only as and through symbols, and in the behavior of people toward these symbols in no way makes them any less vital or "real" from the scientific standpoint. That is, they are items which must be taken into consideration in explaining a given specimen of societal behavior. The gods and the demons are obviously from this point of view in some situations quite as important as policemen and priests in other situations, and hence the former as well as the latter must be dealt with as objective data by sociologists.

Nor do these "cultural," "symbolic," "imaginary" entities represent any special problems because we can deal with all of them in science only symbolically. In sociology, the policeman and the priest as well as the gods become data for science only in their symbolic significance. Their meaning has to be inferred from the behavior of people toward whatever excites their behavior, whether this stimulus be people in uniforms, graven images in stone, totem poles or words. *Symbols representing these meanings as inferred from behavior* are the data of sociological science. (Other sciences may deal with the symbols representing height, weight, and metabolism of policemen and priests.) By overlooking this essential fact, namely, the symbolic nature of the immediate data of all science, the impression of a fundamental difference in the "nature of the subject matter" of different sciences has been created, resulting in an unfortunate neglect in some fields of the powerful methods developed in others.

In the third place, we have noted that one of the scientist's principal problems is to develop a set of symbols in terms of which he can analyze and synthesize the field he has defined. At first he relies on oral symbols consisting of animistic, metaphysical, poetic, and philosophical words. But relationships and situations which are at all complex simply cannot be communicated with any degree of objectivity or accuracy through the spoken word. Science depends almost entirely on written symbols. The relationships and descriptions which scientists wish to communicate are frequently much too complex to be matched in a succession of acoustic stimuli. Consequently the quest is for written symbols which provide an enduring instead of a fleeting stimulus, and offer possibilities of arrangement that cannot be communicated in oral language. In the course of this development we develop rude pictorial or topological representations, i.e., depictions of relationships of connection or position, without metric implications. Geometric, arithmetic, and algebraic ways of expressing relationships usually come with the maturity of every science. The advantages of the latter type of symbol have been pointed out above and in a previous chapter. The more intricate and variable is the situation we wish to describe the more dependent we become upon mathematical systems of symbolization.

Sociology has for some time felt this need. To begin with, this trend took the form of an extensive swing toward the simpler statistical methods in restricted fields where statistical units and data have existed for some time. More recently much work has been done in the development of measuring instruments adapted to societal phenomena hitherto unmetricized. With the rapid developments in this field, the time is ripe for the systematization of the whole field of general sociology in quantitative symbols which, however unique the subject matter to which they refer and however unmetricized as yet some of these phenomena may be, can nevertheless be manipulated according to the already established and tested rules of mathematics.

It will doubtless be observed that in the approach here proposed, in the employment of such terms as fields of force and energy, and especially in the attempt to quantify sociology, we are "imitating" the "physical" sciences. If this statement means that we have been influenced in adopting this approach by its conspicuous success in other sciences, we are, of course, glad to admit such influence. If the coincidence and analogies between the approach here proposed and, for example, the terminology of physics were introduced as *substitutes* for sociological hypotheses and their verification, or as proof of sociological principle there would be legitimate objection to such procedure. But if no such claim is made for them, if they are introduced to stand on their own feet as useful frames of reference for sociological investigation, then the mere *coincidence* that they are also found useful in some other science can in no way be urged as an objection to them, but rather the contrary.

There is no more vicious error present in contemporary sociological thinking than the implied or explicit assumption that the introduction or adaptation of concepts and categories from other sciences constitutes *prima facie* invalid procedure. As a result we not only cut ourselves off from sources of most fruitful hypotheses, but also misguide students into historical and philosophical blind alleys instead of providing them with the technical equipment upon which all modern science relies for verification of its theories. Everyone agrees that the only criterion a scientist needs be concerned about in the development of his theories, methods, and units is their suitability for his purpose. The adoption or adaptation of concepts or methods from other sciences insofar as we find them useful in sociology proceeds entirely from this freedom and flexibility of choice. It is the barring of this "imitation" which constitutes a violation of the principle that data should be organized into *whatever* categories best serve our purposes.

Those who deplore the tendency in the social sciences to "imitate" the other natural sciences overlook that the alternative is to "imitate" some other system of philosophy, theology, or metaphysics. Unless it is assumed that theories come to us through outright revelation, it must be assumed that they come from the accumulated experience of man's life on the earth. Science and scientific methods represent the most generally applicable and reliable residue of that experience. Scientific methods are to an increasing degree accepted as the criterion with respect to which the reliability of all knowledge is gauged. As such, the influence of the other sciences upon sociological thought is not only inevitable but highly desirable.

A certain apparent respectability is imparted to this caution against "imitating" the other sciences by the logical legerdemain of introducing historical cases of such copying, the results of which are no longer valid. What is overlooked is that it was the heavy reliance of Comte, Spencer, and Ward on the concepts of other sciences, *even such as there were at that time,* which made possible the generally conceded contributions of these men. Inasmuch as the physics, biology, and psychology of their day have since undergone revolutionary modifications, it is not to be wondered at if their sociological formulations based on pre-Einsteinian physics and pre-functional behavioristic biology and psychology do not appear to have great utility for present day sociologists. The important fact to bear in mind is that the other sciences, imperfect as they were at the time, still provided an orientation for sociology vastly superior to the then existing methods of talking about societal phenomena.

But there is no need here to enter into an appraisal of the validity of any physical analogies whatsoever, either of the past or the present. No analogies whatever are introduced in this volume to prove a single generalization about societal behavior. What is sought is a set of concepts, categories, and symbols with which to construct a frame of reference within which rigorous logical manipulations of observed facts can be carried on. These concepts, categories, and symbols must be drawn from the best adapted language we have thus far devised for such purposes. If, in casting about for such terms we find various concepts of modern physics, biology, or astronomy, relatively well-adapted to our problem as compared with terms drawn from primitive folklore and ancient philosophy, it should require no apology if we adopt the former. Since the justification for any selection of terms, symbols, and hypotheses which we do make will rest upon the results we get with them, the question of their origin is simply irrelevant.

It may be pointed out in passing that most of the objections to the use of the terminology of other sciences in sociology is simply a reflection of the unfamiliarity of sociologists as to the meaning of these terms even in the sciences where they are admitted to be useful. The delusion is still widespread in sociology that such terms as, for example, atom, electrons, or quanta, energy, force, etc., are small pieces of rock or explosives, or matter of some kind instead of merely words representing convenient observation units of *any* subject matter.[34] In short, if the word atom in the English language means merely an elementary unit of observation, it is as proper for us to use it in sociology as in chemistry. The same can be said for terms such as "satellite" and "constellation" as employed frequently in sociology. They stand not for subject matter but for behavior-relationships. Indeed, it is not only proper to adopt such terms, but necessary for intelligible communication with other scientists. The scientific illiteracy of some contemporary sociologists is hardly sufficient reason for not adopting such parts of the symbolism of other sciences as we find useful, instead of painfully traversing the same ground that they have adequately covered, on the theory that since other scientists find these terms useful, they must *ipso facto* be useless or dangerous in sociology. We have not advocated the opposite procedure as a blind rule, but merely as a permissible step when it serves our purposes.

Finally, critics may remark that in the above terminology and theory we are saying in new terms only what more conventional discussions of the community also say. We have no objection whatever to having it demonstrated that our descriptions in the new terminology coincide with some formulations which other scholars from Aristotle to Cooley have advanced. Indeed, we fully anticipate that this will be found in large degree to be the case. The difference, however, will be that with operational definitions of the concepts and processes described by these men and especially with the mathematical manipulations which these concepts lend themselves to, *demonstration* and *verification* of these theories, and their more rigorous formulation in terms of degree will be possible. On such a foundation, an indefinite extension and growth of sociology might ensue instead of a constant sterile repetition of the pronouncements of seers of the past.

It cannot be emphasized too earnestly that the impasses of science are nearly always solved by a departure from the accepted categories and frames of reference. This does not mean that the existing data or principles are abandoned or destroyed. They merely become special cases of the broader theory and are translated into the new categories required by the new theory. In approaching sociological phenomena as here outlined, we do not propose to ignore any significant observation of community life which previous students, whether ancient or modern, have made. We merely propose to translate these observations into a set of concepts and symbols which lend themselves to a representation of the true position of our observations in a complex so intricate as to be impossible to represent adequately in the language of folklore.

H. Notes

1. See Ch. II, note 3.
2. See W. C. Allee, *Animal Life and Social Growth* (Williams and Wilkins, 1932, Ch. 2), for such descriptions.
3. For further elaboration of this subject see Ch. I, Sec. C, 3. My position is that it is the type of man's reaction rather than any intrinsic

characteristics of phenomena which determines their classification as "cultural," "physical," etc. Very roughly speaking, phenomena which are recognized as human or interhuman behavior and/or the products of such behavior are called "cultural." Which phenomena are reacted to in this special way varies greatly, of course, according to circumstances. But to try to determine whether a phenomenon "really is" a cultural object regardless of anybody's reaction to it, is the kind of metaphysical nonsense I have attacked in the first chapter. (For a revealing summary of such attempts see Albert Blumenthal, "The Nature of Culture," *American Sociological Review,* I, December, 1936, pp. 875-893.)

4. The following description of what constitutes a "field" and a system in another science is illuminating:

"An important characteristic of many of the natural sciences is the concept of a system, for example, the solar system. In order to fix our ideas, we may consider Willard Gibbs' generalized description of a physico-chemical system, which is the basis of a famous contribution to theoretical science that has stood the test of a half century of criticism and use. A physico-chemical system is an isolated material aggregate. It consists of components, which are individual substances, like water or alcohol. These substances are found, singly or together, in phases. Phases are physically homogeneous solid, liquid, or gaseous parts of the system: for example, ice, or a solution of alcohol in water, or air. The system is further characterized by the concentrations of the components in the phases, by its temperature, and by its pressure.

"The reader should note that this description of Gibbs' physico-chemical system is too brief to be rigorous. In particular, a more careful statement of the nature of components and more precise terminology with reference to concentrations are necessary for precision. . . .

"Gibbs' system is plainly a fiction, for no real system can be isolated. Nevertheless, a close approach to isolation, as in a thermos bottle, is possible. So results are obtained and then extended even to systems that are far from isolated. Also, the enumeration of the factors, i.e., concentrations, temperature, and pressure, is incomplete. But it is ordinarily necessary to consider at least these three factors, and sometimes no more need be considered. In other cases the consideration of other factors, like those involved in capillary and electrical phenomena, cannot be avoided. Sometimes, however, such considerations may be introduced after the first analysis in the form of 'corrections.' Finally, the concept is often irrelevant; for instance, the consideration of a watch as a physico-chemical system would be a waste of time.

"It need hardly be said that such apparent defects are in truth consequences of very real advantages. They are but signs of the well-chosen simplifications and abstractions that make possible a systematic treatment of complex phenomena. This instrument that Gibbs has put in the chemists' service has immeasurably advanced the science of chemistry: it has clarified, directed, and economized the thought of all chemists. It enables us to understand, for example, refrigeration, the manufacture of steel, and the respiratory function of the blood.

"The central feature of Pareto's General Sociology is the construction of a similar conceptual scheme: the social system. This possesses many of the same logical advantages and limitations that are present in the physico-chemical system. Pareto's social system contains individuals; they are roughly analogous to Gibbs' components. It is heterogeneous (cf. Gibbs' phases), for the individuals are of different families, trades, and professions; they are associated with different institutions and are members of different economic and social classes. As Gibbs considers temperature, pressure, and concentrations, so Pareto considers sentiments, or, strictly speaking, the manifestations of sentiments in words and deeds, verbal elaborations, and the economic interests. Like Gibbs, Pareto excludes many factors that are important in special cases, but he too has demonstrated that he can do much within the limitations that he has chosen, and that such limitations are necessary." (L. J. Henderson, *Pareto's General Sociology,* Harvard University Press, 1935, pp. 10-11, 15, 16.)

5. There was at the time the First Edition was written, and there still remains, great confusion in the use of certain terms denoting conceptual schemes with which man approaches, and according to which he organizes, his observations and experiences. Consider the following list of such conceptual schemes (words and phrases): definition, hypothesis, theory, model, axiom, postulate, law, principle, frame of reference, Weltanschauung, word-map, conceptual scheme, universe of discourse. J. B. Conant (*On Understanding Science*) has called attention to the ambiguity of the words "hypothesis" and "theory" as follows: "The reader may be reminded that the words *theory* and *hypothesis* are frequently employed to describe both conceptual schemes and models, or pictures, 'explaining' such schemes. A discussion of the definition of theory and hypothesis is often given in elementary texts, but I think such consideration of doubtful value. Because of the ambiguity, it is well, perhaps, to avoid as far as possible both words in discussing the evolution of science." (Pp. 57-58.) And further: "I have avoided the use of the word theory except where it has become an accepted part of the language of science as 'kinetic theory of gases' and the 'phlogiston theory.' The words concept and conceptual scheme seem to me much preferable to the use of the words hypothesis and theory." (Pp. 136-137.)

I find that for my purposes Conant's suggestion is a good one not only as regards "theory" and "hypothesis" but also for most of the other words and phrases given in the list above. The problem has been discussed with much perspicacity by Hans L. Zetterberg in his *On Theory and Verification in Sociology* (Almquist and Wiksell, Stockholm, 1954. The Tressler Press, p. 27). A more rigorous definition of each of the words and phrases in the above list is, of course, desirable. Some discussion of the matter will be found on the following pages of the First Edition: 3-6, 8-9, 73, 100-102, 112-113, 115-117, 135, 148, 151-152.

6. Consider, for example, the present situation in physics regarding the wave theory and the corpuscular theory of light. See A. Einstein and L. Infeld, *The Evolution of Physics,* Simon and Schuster, 1938, p. 278.

7. W. I. Thomas, *Primitive Behavior,* McGraw-Hill, 1937, p. 8.

8. In taking this view, we are not forgetting the position we have taken in the first chapter with respect to the unity of scientific method regardless of the subject matter to which it is applied. We agree that within the scientific framework and for most general purposes all observable behavior must be regarded as consisting of transformations of energy whether the behavior takes place in a test tube, a gasoline engine, an organism, or in the United States Senate. Now the sciences that deal with the subject of energy-transformation in its most general form might from this point of view be regarded as fundamental to those sciences which deal in a more restricted way, that is, with special types, forms, or cases of energy transformation. It is unquestionably of advantage to workers in the more restricted fields to know the more general laws of energy transformation (and *vice versa*) and as a matter of fact, all workers in the more specialized fields probably do have such knowledge, however informally they have come by it and however unaware they may be of possessing it. This is the knowledge they refer to and summarize as the "nature" of the behaving entity. Even if we reduce a phenomenon to atoms, electrons, or quanta, we have to say in the end that it is the "nature" of quanta to behave as they do. But it does not follow that the phenomena of special fields must be reduced for purposes of the special field to the most refined and abstract formulations of atomic physics. (An excellent discussion of the reductionist fallacy will be found in Read Bain, "The Concept of Complexity in Sociology II," *Social Forces,* VIII, March, 1930, pp. 374 ff. For a good statement of an opposing viewpoint, see M. King Hubbert, "The Place of Geophysics in a Department of Geology," *American Institute of Mining and Metallurgical Engineers, Technical Publication No. 945* (1938).) On the contrary, this would frequently be no explanation at all of some questions to which answers are desired. A thorough understanding of the physics of all the motions involved in the behavior called marriage would not constitute the type of explanation of this phenomenon which the sociologist desires and needs in order to make societal predictions. Some phenomena are explained

through analytic procedures involving breaking it up into parts, components, or factors. Others are just as truly explained through synthetic procedures involving the placing of a part in a larger scheme. Which procedure we adopt in a given case depends entirely upon the problem (the nature of the tension) with which we start out.

This question arises most frequently in sociology in connection with its alleged dependency upon psychology. Pursuing a mystical notion of "causation" and "explanation," a large number of sociologists have been at one time or another smitten with the notion that to "explain" sociological phenomena they must "reduce" them to psychological phenomena, which must in turn be reduced to biological, then to physico-chemical terms, and then (presumably) back to God, the craving for Whom is doubtless at the bottom of the quest for this type of "cause" and "explanation." (For a philosophical discussion of the subject see E. Nagel, "The Logic of Reduction in the Sciences," *Erkenntnis,* V, Aug.-Sept., 1935, pp. 46-51.) The viewpoint still has some adherents and the question occasionally recurs in discussions regarding the "group fallacy" which we shall mention in a later chapter. In the meantime, as "physical" scientists themselves are becoming more aware of the nature of their own explanations and more modest about its "ultimate" nature, it is being realized that the only explanation known in science is conceptualized description and that this may be as complete and objective on the sociological level in sociological terms as any formulation of physics or chemistry. An accurate statement of all the *sociological* conditions under which marriage occurs with a stated degree of probability, is as full and scientific an explanation of the *sociological* aspect of this phenomenon, as the statement of all the physico-chemical conditions attending a given type of explosion is an explanation of the physico-chemical aspects of the latter phenomenon. But an explosion may have sociological aspects which would in no way be explained by the physico-chemical analysis. Both types of events may be analyzed indefinitely from all points of view, i.e., in all their aspects. But explanation is not an absolute. It is always and entirely relative to the question we want answered. If that question is in sociological terms the answer must also be in these terms. The particular explanation which we desire in a given case will vary with the specific problem we have in mind. The latter will vary according to what we already know. An explanation which fully satisfies a child will frequently not satisfy an adult. Explanations of the cosmos and of man's origin which were regarded as entirely satisfactory at one time do not satisfy today as explanations. In short, we need not look for final or eternal explanations of anything. What constitutes an explanation will always be relative to the inquiring organism, and the frames of reference within which that organism is accustomed to function. Explanation is, therefore, a word we use to describe our feeling when some new phenomenon has been classified under some already familiar category so that our curiosity regarding the former comes to rest. It is not a mysterious key lying hidden somewhere in nature which if we "search" diligently we may "discover" and then know the "true" explanation of a phenomenon for all time. (See also note 3, Ch. I.)

9. J. A. Thomson and P. Geddes, *Life: Outlines of General Biology,* Harper, 1932, II, p. 1240.

10. W. M. Malisoff, "Arranging the Sciences: I. An Experiment," *Philosophy of Science,* IV, Apr., 1937, p. 263.

11. P. A. Sorokin, "Sociology as a Science," *Social Forces,* X, Oct., 1931, pp. 23-24. (Chart on p. 26.)

12. For one thing, the scientific theory which I have said is desirable, must itself be drawn from the accumulated experience of the race, the bulk of which must always be in the form of largely unrelated records of local adjustments made for immediate purposes. I am not deploring this type of research or advocating its abandonment. This reservation is all the more necessary here on account of the current practice in sociological discussion of assuming that if a person advocates some one approach he is *ipso facto* against all others. I therefore categorically state that, while I advocate the conduct of systematic research directed by integrated theory instead of isolated and vagrant hypotheses, I also warmly favor (1) random observation, (2) systematic exploration, (3) testing of isolated hypotheses, and (4) any procedure whatever which yields results relevant to human adjustments. Under the limitation of certain definitions, I may be compelled to call all of these alternative procedures unscientific or nonscientific. But this is not necessarily a derogation of them. (I have elsewhere elaborated this subject; see "Is Sociology Too Scientific?" *Sociologus,* IX, Sept., 1933, pp. 298-320. For an excellent discussion of the criteria of science as compared with *other forms of knowledge,* see also J. Michael and M. Adler, *Crime, Law, and Social Science,* Harcourt, 1932, pp. 44-76.)

13. See the excellent discussion by J. F. Brown ("On the Use of Mathematics in Psychological Theory," *Psychometrika,* I, March, 1936, pp. 79-82) of the concept of the psychological field which applies equally well to the sociological field as here used. See also note 21 below.

"There is always a *field* in which observations of *this* or *that* object or event occur. Observation of the latter is made for the sake of finding out what that *field* is with reference to some active adaptive response to be made in carrying forward a *course* of behavior." (John Dewey, *Logic. The Theory of Inquiry,* Holt, 1938, p. 67.)

14. This is a position which has been much emphasized in recent years by Gestalt psychologists, although they have shown a tendency to make fallacious assumptions regarding the nature of the "situation as a whole."

(See G. A. Lundberg, "Quantitative Methods in Social Psychology," *Amer. Sociol. Rev.*, Feb., 1936, pp. 44-50.) The position has also been emphasized for some decades by sociologists, e.g., in the writings of W. I. Thomas and L. L. Bernard. A brief statement of the field-theoretical position here taken will be found in G. A. Lundberg, "The Demographic and Economic Basis of Political Radicalism and Conservatism," *Amer. Jour. Sociol.*, XXXII, March, 1927, pp. 724-725 (footnote). See also S. A. Rice, *Quantitative Methods in Politics*, Knopf, 1928, Chs. 1-3. For a fuller application of the theory, see G. A. Lundberg, "Public Opinion from a Behavioristic Viewpoint," *Amer. Jour. Sociol.*, XXXVI, Nov., 1930, pp. 387-405. By far the fullest and ablest exposition of the theory as well as applications of it to sociology will be found in J. F. Brown, *Psychology and the Social Order*, McGraw-Hill, 1936.

15. Cf. R. Mukerjee, "The Regional Balance of Man," *Amer. Jour. Sociol.*, XXXVI, Nov., 1930. "Perhaps the most important contribution of ecology is the idea of the region as an intricate network of interrelations. . . . In the older sociological speculation man was treated as a part of nature, but in a frankly deterministic fashion; his plans and endeavors were conceived more as extraneous forces than as phases of the ecologic complex interwoven with the rest of the environment. Man is part and parcel of the process by which the balance of the region is maintained or shifted. . . ." (Pp. 455-456.) Cf. also A. F. Bentley, "Sociology and Mathematics," *Sociological Review*, XXXIII, Oct., 1931.

16. See Ch. VIII, Section C, of the First Edition, for elaboration of this point.

17. For a development of this position, namely, that tangibility, concreteness, etc., are not characteristics inherent in data but merely words describing the degree to which we have developed objective symbolic technics of dealing with such data, see G. A. Lundberg, "The Thoughtways of Contemporary Sociology," *Amer. Sociol. Rev.*, I, Oct., 1936, pp. 703-723. See also A. F. Bentley, *Behavior Knowledge Fact*, Principia Press, 1935. Chs. 19, 21.

18. See C. R. Shaw, *Delinquency Areas*, University of Chicago Press, 1929. Elsa S. Longmoor and E. F. Young, "Ecological Interrelationships of Juvenile Delinquency and Population Mobility," *Amer. Jour. Sociol.*, XLI, March, 1936, pp. 598-610.

19. See J. F. Brown, *Psychology and the Social Order*, McGraw-Hill, 1936, pp. 476 ff. Also K. Lewin, *Principles of Topological Psychology*, McGraw-Hill, 1936, Pt. II; and especially Dodd's *Dimensions of Society*, Macmillan, 1940.

20. The term correlation is here used in its broadest sense. See G. A. Lundberg, "Quantitative Methods in Social Psychology," *Amer. Sociol. Rev.*, I, Feb., 1936, pp. 41-43. See also Ch. II, Sections C and D.

21. We use the term "social space" in the Riemannian sense, i.e., as a mathematical (geometric) construct defined as a manifold in which positional relationships of *any kind* may be expressed. From this point of view we may employ spatial constructs to depict relationships quite independent of direction or distance. These may be relationships of connection, position, or any other properties of a qualitative, nonmetrical nature. According to Riemann, spaces may be constructed of any dimensions and properties provided they are logically consistent. He also showed that the properties of a space may be dependent upon the dynamics of processes within that space. Topology, as the geometry of such spaces, may therefore be of great importance to sociology as a solution of the controversy over quantitative *vs.* qualitative methods. That is, qualitative (as yet nonmetricized) relationships may through topological constructs be rendered about as objective as quantitative or metrical constructs. If so, present objections to qualitative operations and terms would disappear. The use of spatial constructs and terms with reference to social relationships is, of course, very ancient and merely reflects the fact that relational thinking tends to structure itself in spatial terms. (Cf. J. F. Brown, "On the Use of Mathematics in Psychological Theory," *Psychometrika,* I, March, 1936, pp. 77-90. See also P. A. Sorokin, *Social Mobility,* Harpers, 1927, Ch. II, for a good nonmathematical statement of the same point.) Algebraic description should, of course, supersede the geometric as soon as possible.

22. As an illustration of the ambiguity of the language used in current sociological discussion see my discussion, *Amer. Jour. Sociol.,* XLII, March, 1937, of an article by H. E. Jensen and Mr. Jensen's reply, in which he insists that his article means to him exactly the opposite of what it means to me. For another conspicuous illustration see the controversy between John Dewey and R. M. Hutchins, in *The Social Frontier,* III, Feb.-March, 1937.

For an excellent brief treatise on the nature of mathematical expressions, their importance and the impossibility of translating some of them into folk language or of making them vehicles of "intuitive understanding," see R. Carnap, "Foundations of Logic and Mathematics," *International Encyclopedia of Unified Science,* I, No. 3, especially pp. 44, 47, 60, 64-69. See also L. Bloomfield, "Linguistic Aspects of Science," *ibid.,* No. 4.

23. Einstein and Infeld, *op. cit.,* p. 226.

24. C. H. Cooley seems to have had some such thought in mind when he said:

"There is no way to penetrate the surface of life but by attacking it earnestly at a particular point. If one takes his stand in a field of corn when the young plants have begun to sprout, all the plants in the field will appear to be arranged in a system of rows radiating from his feet; and no matter where he stands the system will appear to centre at that point. It is so with any standpoint in the field of thought and intercourse; to possess it is to have a point of vantage from which the whole may, in a particular manner, be apprehended. It is surely a matter of common observation that a man who knows no one thing intimately has no views worth hearing on things in general." (C. H. Cooley, *Human Nature and the Social Order*, Scribners, 1902, p. 117.)

25. See, for example, L. L. Thurstone, *Vectors of Mind*, University of Chicago Press, 1935.

26. L. J. Henderson, *Pareto's General Sociology*, Harvard University Press, 1935, pp. 110, 111. Henderson's analysis of the process of scientific theory construction in terms of "steps" should not be taken too literally to imply a discrete series or order in time. Actually, the process goes forward as a whole.

27. *Ibid.*, pp. 107, 108.

28. The best example of these attempts is perhaps to be found in Wm. McDougall, *Social Psychology*, J. W. Luce, 1911.

29. W. G. Sumner and A. G. Keller, *The Science of Society*, Yale University Press, 1927, I, Chs. 1, 2.

30. W. I. Thomas, *op. cit.*, Ch. 3.

31. See P. Geddes and J. A. Thomson, *Biology*, pp. 139, 178-179, 237-238, 242. Also A. F. Bentley, "Sociology and Mathematics," *Sociological Review*, XXIII, Oct., 1931.

32. A recent study has analyzed seven sociological theories and theorists from a common point of view. (Charles P. and Zona K. Loomis, *Modern Social Theories*, Van Nostrand, 1961.) The Epilogue of the present volume attempts a comparison of two such systems.

33. For a fuller exposition of this point see Chapters VI and XII of the First Edition as to the meaning of environment in sociology.

34. Cf. W. M. Malisoff, "What Is an Atom?" *Philosophy of Science*, VI, July, 1939, pp. 261-265: "A tree can be an atom in an atomistic analysis of a forest, so long as its structure is not in question, i.e., its structure is non-existent in the context of the given analysis. This, incidentally, takes the wind out of the sails of the navigators of this theoretical sea, who propose to distinguish an atom from a tree, on the basis of the tree being a simple perception and the atom being a 'construct.' Some atoms may be too large to be seen. It is the difficulty of the demonstration of the *meaning* that varies. It is easy to *point* to a tree, it requires much more pointing to point out a chemical atom. The difficulty, however, has nothing to do with the character of being an atom in a given analysis." (P. 265.) See also W. V. Metcalf, "The Reality of the Atom," *Philosophy of Science, op. cit.*, pp. 367-371.

Chapter IV

SOCIOLOGICAL LAWS

A. The Meaning of Law in Science

THE VIEWPOINT DEVELOPED in the preceding chapters has been adopted because it is the most convenient approach compatible with the generally accepted goal of all science. That goal is the formulation of valid and verifiable principles or laws comprehending with the greatest parsimony all the phenomena of that aspect of the cosmos which is under consideration. Since this is in science the crucial test of all points of views and procedures, it is desirable to summarize in this chapter the meaning of law in science, with special reference to the possibility of developing such generalizations for societal phenomena.

It is our thesis that the term "scientific law" can and should mean in the social sciences exactly what it means in any of the other sciences. There seems to be considerable agreement among scientists as well as others that a scientific law is a generalized and verifiable statement, within measurable degrees of accuracy, of how certain events occur under stated conditions. More specifically then, a scientific law is (1) a group of verbal or mathematical symbols (2) designating an unlimited number of defined events in terms of a limited number of reactions (3) so that the performance of specified operations always yields predictable results (4) within measurable limits.

B. Types of Laws

TWO TYPES OR DEGREES of generalization are usually included and sometimes confused under the rubric *scientific law*. One type merely states the statistical probability of the occurrence of an event under stated conditions. The other type, more common in sociology, is a tautological statement in which the conclusion stated is inherent in the definition of the words employed. Thus, the "law" of inertia, to the effect that matter will remain at rest unless some force acts upon it, follows from the definition of force as *that which* produces motion.[1] That is, the law is a truism and requires on this level no empirical demonstration because it follows from the postulate and definition of force, and the definition of inertia as the state of matter in the absence of force. Such a law or verbal axiom may often be applied with as much validity to societal as to other phenomena. Comte's statement that "Kepler's law of inertia . . . is merely a particular case of the tendency of all natural phenomena to persevere in their state unless disturbed," [2] is obviously entirely sound because the conclusion follows from the definition of the terms used. That is, the statement amounts to saying that phenomena remain undisturbed unless disturbed. Within the framework selected, under the adopted postulate of force and its definition, it is logically irrefutable to say that all societies, institutions, customs, or societal behavior will remain as they are unless acted upon by some force. The practical uses of such a generalization in any field depends entirely upon our ability to estimate the relative probabilities of various hypothetical possibilities.

The same is true of such a generalization as Spencer's law that social motion follows the line of least resistance. If the line of least resistance is determined, as it must be, from the observation that some individual or group does act in a certain way rather than in a number of other theoretically possible ways, and if the observed behavior is regarded as the sole evidence of the line of least resistance, the generalization obviously follows. Nor is the law in any way invalidated by instances of men, unsuspected of a crime, giving themselves up "voluntarily" and, as the popular version has it, "choosing the more difficult path." The latter statement is clearly based on some definition of "line of least resistance" other than that employed above. Another illustration is Ward's "law" that individuals seek the greatest gain at the least cost. If relative gain and cost are considered as defined, measured, and demonstrated by the fact that the observed behavior, rather than some theoretical alternatives, took place, the conclusion undoubtedly follows, for the "law" is a truism.

Such truisms, or axioms, may have value in giving framework and direction to investigation.[3] A distinction should therefore be made between scientific tautologies and those which the dictionaries define as *"needless* or *useless* repetition of the same ideas in different words." The practical value of scientific tautologies depends entirely upon the possibility of deducing from them theorems which correctly describe the behavior of large numbers of concrete observed events. The objective demonstration that these theorems do describe the events, waits upon the developments of measuring devices for the standardization of human responses so that individuals can corroborate or refute each other's observations. Which postulate out of many possible ones are finally adopted depends solely upon their relative capacity to cover large numbers of cases with convenience and without inconsistency. That is, they are judged on the principles of parsimony, convenience, and consistency. The transition in the social sciences, notably since Darwin, in the direction of the other sciences is merely a quest for axioms from which societal as well as "physical" events can be deduced, thus obviating the need for a double set of axioms, one covering social, the other "physical," events. Such a quest may, of course, just as readily call for modification in the theoretical framework of the "physical" sciences as in the social.

The practical usefulness of either of the generalizations given above, and of others like them in all sciences, depends upon the possibility of developing devices for measuring "social resistance," "gain," and "loss." When such devices are developed any number of cases of resistance to a given social motion or change, as well as to alternative changes, can be measured and the degree of the alleged correlation can thus be determined. In the case of Spencer's "law" the problem would be to find reliable criteria of social resistance which can be standardized into an instrument of measurement (i.e., device for standardizing human responses). Such a measure should enable us to predict the likelihood that a change will be in one direction rather than another from the fact that the measured resistance to one change was less than to any of the others.

The axiom itself does not give us this essential information. It has to be secured through a careful analysis of empirical facts. It is this verifiable conclusion thus induced in terms of measured units, by which actual prediction of concrete events can be made, which constitutes the true scientific law. Until the generalization is thus successfully subjected to empirical test it is a verbal truism, or axiom, rather than a law. Most sociological generalizations have not yet been verified by the empirical test. Before they can be so tested the terms in which they are couched must be reduced to repeatable operations of some kind so that the behavior from which such categories as "resistance," "gain," or "loss" are inferred, can be checked by different individuals, and the postulated presence of the "forces" related to specified changes.

The development of sociological laws as defined above clearly calls for this indispensable development of instruments for more rigid and objective definition of the terms in which present generalizations are couched and especially the relating of these terms to concrete behavior. Consider such "laws" as the following: "All growth of personality in the members of a community involves a correspondent change in their relations to one another, in the social structure, in the customs, institutions, and associations of community." [4] A briefer statement of the same "law" by the same author is "The differentiation of community is relative to the growth of personality in social individuals." [5] What is needed here is an objective measure of "differentiation" and of "growth of personality," not to mention "community." The compulsion to define such terms in observable behavior-segments would doubtless in itself lead to illuminating results, possibly even necessitating the abandonment of such a term as personality for scientific purposes. Until the "law" can be thus stated in terms of objective units referring to actual behavior, it is not susceptible of either proof or disproof, except, of course, insofar as it is a truism in which "growth of personality" and "differentiation of community" are defined in terms of each other. As stated above, this has some value in giving direction and a frame to investigation. The ultimate end is the correlation of two disparate sets of behavior phenomena so that the statement of their relationship will be consistent with sense experience. Only when standardized symbolic instruments for the observation and measurement of these behavior phenomena are developed can the generalization be put to empirical test, and prediction be made.

Many thousands of "laws" of the type exemplified above could
adily be assembled. They would range from the most trivial proverb
ch as "the voice with the smile wins" or "honesty is the best policy"
generalizations of cosmic scope. We have noted above that most
these laws are not in their present form susceptible to empirical
rification. In addition, and taken as a whole, they lack one other
quirement of useful scientific laws. This is their lack of relation-
ip. Petty generalizations regarding local affairs are inextricably
ixed up with broad generalizations purporting to be valid for human
ciety as a whole. There is frequently no systematic attempt even
the same author to relate his various generalizations and to derive
em from a limited number of basic concepts. Such a synthesis must,
course, spring from the accretion of a multitude of minor gen-
alizations and there is here no desire to disparage the somewhat
aotic work which has been done. On the other hand, the principle
parsimony and consistency with other known scientific laws, must
ways be an important consideration in science. The achievements of
ience in this respect is one of the principal measures of its advance-
ent. Accordingly, unity, coherence, and integration of generaliza-
ons, as well as the multiplicity of their applications, must be the
eal sought.

C. Obstacles to the Development of Sociological Laws

VE HAVE REVIEWED in preceding chapters the more common mis-
pprehensions regarding the possibility of arriving at reliable scien-
fic laws of societal phenomena because of the alleged subjectivity,
eterogeneity, complexity, and nonmeasurability of these phenomena.
s one writer has quaintly put it, "social scientists . . . set for them-
elves the paradoxical ambition to be objective about the subjective
spects of life." [6] The same statement as regards homogeneity, com-
lexity, and measurability would constitute a very adequate sum-
nary of the position which we repudiate. According to the view cited
bove, objectivity and subjectivity, as well as homogeneity, com-
lexity, and measurability and their opposites are given in the data.
he Lord not only created the data but clearly labeled them unmis-
akably as to objectivity, measurability, homogeneity, and so forth.

We have repeatedly pointed out in preceding chapters the untenabili
of such an assumption in a scientific universe of discourse. Obje
tivity, measurability, homogeneity, complexity, etc., must, under t
postulates on which science proceeds, be regarded not as inhere
characteristics of phenomena but as designations of man's ways
responding and communicating his responses.

Consider, for example, the specious illustration which points
the "law" that "water" freezes at 32°F as evidence of the invaria
validity of the laws of physics as a result of the "stability" of "phys
cal" subject matter. What would become of the reliability of this la
if water were not first defined as H_2O instead of including under th
word all fluids that our unaided senses identify as water, and if i
stead of a thermometer's reading of temperatures, the subjective est
mates of different individuals were accepted? "Water" would, und
these conditions, "freeze" under such apparently varied "temper
tures" as to make the law as unreliable as most sociological laws a
today. The homogeneity of H_2O resides precisely in the abstraction
these elements, as contrasted with the full heterogeneity of all t
liquids that are called water in daily discourse. The heterogeneity
societal data at present resides in the relative crudeness of the cat
gories we employ to delimit and designate societal observations.

Another obstacle which is supposed to be especially insurmoun
able in the development of sociological laws is the alleged imposs
bility of controlled experiment—"to exclude all irrelevant factors ar
to control all relevant factors." [7] This objection comes near to statir
the principal shortcoming of the social sciences today, namely, the
inability to measure and therefore to "control" the various conditio
that influence social behavior. There are two ways in which this co
trol can be achieved: (1) by laboratory elimination of the disturbir
influences (e.g., vacuum chambers, glasses eliminating certain ligl
rays, etc.) or (2) by measuring these influences so that allowanc
can be made for their influence in the observed results. The reserva
tion of "other things being equal" is not the serious drawback whic
it is generally assumed to be, nor is it unique in the social science
As we have frequently pointed out, all scientific laws stipulate und
what conditions the reported sequence occurs and implicitly or ex
plicitly the degree of probability of their occurrence under these co
ditions. The really serious difference between this situation and th
which obtains in the laws of social science today is that the latter d

ot know *what* conditions and *what* degrees thereof they include
nder the reservation "other things being equal." Only when these
onditions are known and measured do we have a scientific law as de-
ned in this volume.

It is by virtue of this knowledge that the other sciences can con-
ol, or what amounts to the same thing, allow for, the operation of
ese conditions, both in the laboratory and especially in the practical
pplications of these laws toward the objects of human striving. The
ontrol of altitude and air pressure in a demonstration of the law of
lling bodies comes only after we know that these factors influence
e behavior in question. The usefulness of this law, for example in
he calculation of the path of a projectile or other practical use, de-
ends upon our ability to *measure* to what extent these conditions in
given practical situation influence the event. Without the knowledge
f what conditions influence the behavior described by a law, the
ecessary laboratory conditions cannot be set up and the law cannot
e formulated. Without methods of measuring to what degree con-
itions in actual practical situations deviate from those laboratory
onditions, the law is useless for practical purposes. Actually, of
ourse, the knowledge of the conditions that influence the behavior
escribed by the law means some kind of measurement of these con-
itions. The most conspicuous defect of most present "social laws"
, as stated before, precisely this: *We do not know under what spe-
ific conditions they are true and to what degree they are verifi-
bly true under these conditions.* This defect can be remedied in
ocial as in physical science only by the development of technics of
measurement.

Closely related to the above objections, if indeed not implicit in
hem, is the feeling that sociological laws must always be relative
o a specific culture and therefore can never have the general validity
f laws in, for example, physics. This objection flows perhaps even
nore from a common misapprehension of the laws of physics than
rom misconceptions regarding the nature of sociological laws. What
s usually referred to as the laws of physics in this connection are the
xioms or truisms considered above. They owe their universality as
ve have seen to the logical syntax of the language in which they are
tated, not to any empirical reference. To say that a body will remain
t rest unless disturbed is like saying that a person without contacts
vill be isolated. When it comes to laws with empirical references, the

laws of physics are not only rigidly circumscribed in their applicability, they usually describe behavior as it occurs *nowhere* in the
natural, uncontrolled universe, but under laboratory conditions such
as, for example, in a vacuum, under the assumption of no friction, or
under other ideal or theoretical conditions. The universality of their
practical application flows from the refined measuring instruments
that have been devised for measuring the *degree to which actual
natural situations deviate from* the ideal conditions specified in the
formal statement of the law. Except for these measurements, physics
would have to have a separate law for every altitude and every wind
velocity. In short, every community would have its own laws of
physics, as it is now sometimes contended that every cultural group
must have its own sociological laws. The remedy for the latter situation is clearly the same as has already been applied in the former
namely, the selection of social behavior phenomena so general as to
be present in all cultures (e.g., Le Play's "Folk, Work, and Place")
and deriving from these universal phenomena measures of variation
describing *in the same basic categories* all variations thereof.

Such attempts have, indeed, been made in the social sciences. The
concept of the "economic man," for example, was such an ideal construct. The trouble with this construct was not that such abstraction
is inherently fallacious, but in the forgetfulness of its creators that
this was an ideal construct and in their consequent failure to develop
the necessary methods of measuring the deviation of the various concrete existing economic men and situations from their ideal construct
of a theoretical economic man on an isolated island. No opinion is
here expressed as to the value of this particular construct as a norm
from which to measure deviations. I am using it only as an illustration of a method of procedure which is inevitable in science, because
it is intimately related to the principle of parsimony. The alternative
is a law for every situation, which is a negation of the meaning of
law in science. The central problem is how to standardize a set of social situations so that deviations from them in standardized terms can
be most conveniently measured, i.e., so that prediction can be made
when the degree of deviation of conditions in a concrete situation
from those of the ideal situation are known.

In the absence of the possibility of laboratory control, as is perhaps inevitable in most sociological inquiry, the establishment of statistical norms and the accurate measurement of variations around these norms achieves the same purpose in measurable degrees. It is a commonplace that a statistical mean frequently does not correspond to or correctly describe a single item in the series averaged, just as it has been pointed out that the "economic man" of the economists does not correspond exactly to a single one of the millions of men on the earth. The mean is nevertheless a powerful device for describing, and with its ancillary methods, for predicting and estimating probabilities. Much of the criticism of economic theories involving the "economic man" has been justified because some of the theorists employing the concept, as well as their critics, have assumed it to represent something which it could not possibly represent. They have accordingly engaged in much irrelevant discussion. But to assume that science can get along without type-concepts or abstractions of this sort is as vain as to assume we can get along in science without means, "ideal types," and other statistical devices. In fact, many sociologists are inclined to forget that physicists are at their best when they report the behavior of specially manufactured balls rolling down perfectly smooth planes in vacuum chambers, etc. They do not fill their books with innumerable anecdotes about stones rolling down actual mountains in different parts of the world. Concepts of "normal," "other things equal," etc., are as essential in the social sciences as in other sciences.

Consider, in this connection, the following poser by Boulding: "If the heavenly bodies were themselves moved by astronomers, or even if they were moved by temperamental angels who guided their behavior by the astronomers' predictions, astronomers would find themselves in just as bad a fix as the economists. The bacteriologist who must stain his bacteria in order to see them would be in even worse trouble if his bacteria blushed when they were observed." [8] At first glance, this appears to be one of the most apparent and plausible differences between the social and the physical sciences. But is it a significant or fatal difference of the type alleged? Suppose the astronomers could move the heavenly bodies by derricks or magnets as the scientists can manipulate the materials and the animals of their laboratories. Would it not increase rather than decrease their power of scientific study of these phenomena? Such power would make astronomy an experimental science like physics. As for bacteria (or girls) that blush when they are observed, three solutions long since invented by scientists seem applicable: (1) devise methods of observing under which the observed is not aware of it (e.g., one-way glass in nursery schools, etc.); (2) develop indifference to observation on the part of the observed (e.g., laboratory animals, including children, communities frequently surveyed, etc.); (3) discover and measure exactly what difference in behavior results from being observed, and allow for this difference in our correlations and conclusions (e.g., it has been discovered what difference altitude makes in the law of falling bodies, and we can therefore usefully employ the law at all altitudes).

In short, all laboratory experimentation is open to the objection above urged against the social sciences. The essence of experimentation is for the experimenter to possess the very powers that Boulding fears would raise havoc in astronomy. In justice to the author, it should be mentioned that he makes the following reservation: "Of course not even the astronomer seems to be exempt from observer trouble in these days of relativity." [9] But it is not necessary to take advantage of these more recondite considerations in order to make the point at issue. Do we not *intentionally* "influence" the behavior of the white rat when we set up an experiment to study its behavior? Both the design of the experiment and the fact that we observe the rat's behavior are bound to affect that behavior. It might be argued, after the manner of the economist who objects to the study of "artificial" situations, that we are interested in the behavior of rats in their natural habitats and that the study of them under highly artificial laboratory conditions, therefore, is either unimportant or misleading. No one ever raises this point because it is well known that we learn very important things about rats (and other animals), including knowledge of vast importance in understanding rat behavior in its natural habitat, from the study of rats in laboratories. How can this be? Our studies enable us to arrive at *principles—abstract generalizations of general validity* that are applicable to large varieties of special cases. The whole manner of speaking about the observer being part of what he observes is obviously ambiguous and imprecise. In logic or in any rigorous manner of speaking, things are "part of" whatever categories we set up and whatever classifications we choose to make. Scientific laws apply, in any case, only to stipulated conditions, and it is for the scientist to select and to stipulate these conditions.

There remains what to many appears to be the crucial case: What about heavenly bodies controlled by temperamental angels whose behavior is modified by the very fact of the astronomers' predictions? A presidential address to the social science section of the AAAS some years ago put the matter this way: "One can talk about nature without disturbing nature, but one cannot talk about society without changing in some measure the whole course of social development." Is it not a fact that the behavior of people may be affected by the very generalizations and predictions made by social scientists about that behavior? It certainly is a fact. But what of it?

To deal first with the angels, it may be noted that astronomy seems to have achieved a very considerable development during centuries when it was, in fact, believed that the heavenly bodies, as well as other physical phenomena, were in a high degree controlled by precisely such temperamental angels. This did not deter men from observing, recording, and generalizing about certain regularities in the "temperament" of the angels.[10] Later scientists dispensed with the postulate that the regularities and the irregularities of natural phenomena were attributable to the whims of angels, but they continued to observe with increasing care and accuracy the regularities and the irregularities.

Since man is the only animal that employs to any considerable extent language and symbols, it is true that language, in the form of scientific predictions and otherwise, becomes a part of the environment which influences human behavior. But man's speech is merely one of the forms of his behavior which modify the world in which he lives. Engineering works influence the course of rivers, and vaccines influence the behavior of bacteria, as compared with their behavior before the scientist interfered with their "natural" courses or ways of life. As is well known, bacteria develop immunities or make adaptations to the new conditions imposed upon them by scientists. Does this destroy or make impossible a science of bacteriology? No, for the modified behavior itself becomes the object of further study by scientists.

Finally, consider the following apparently fundamental difference between physical and social prediction: "If Galileo says that two cannon balls of unequal size dropped simultaneously from the Leaning Tower of Pisa will hit the ground at the same time, his prophecy does not affect the outcome of the experiment. But statements about human relations are not like physical statements." [11] *In what respect* are the two kinds of statements "different"? Certainly they are different in subject matter. Human individuals and groups are unique in that they are influenced by their own and others' speech, including predictions. Cannon balls are definitely not so influenced. But the two kinds of statement are definitely similar in that each must take into consideration all the relevant and important influences producing the behavior studied in each case. The different sciences are largely differentiated on this basis, namely, the similarity or difference of the subject matter or problems in which they are interested. But within a given subject matter, the procedure for arriving at such statements are everywhere the same. The so-called "self-fulfilling prophecy," noted by social scientists, is merely a designation of the undoubted fact that prediction of social events *may be* among the influences producing (or avoiding) the predicted behavior. To determine the likelihood and the degree of such influence at work under various circumstances is, of course, a legitimate and important concern of social scientists. Other scientists study other influences that operate among the phenomena with which they are concerned.

For example, altitude has been found to be one of the conditions that influence the rate of speed with which bodies fall. The cooperation of a group of people (a social phenomenon) may not be influenced at all by altitude. But they are influenced by speech and discussion whether it takes the form of modifying their behavior as a result of the impassioned harangue of a leader, or as a result of the sober prediction of a social scientist that *unless* the group takes such and such action, certain consequences will very probably ensue. *All* behavior is influenced by *certain* conditions, which may not observably or significantly affect other behavior. *To find out what these significant influences are* for specified types of behavior and *how they operate to bring about or modify other behavior* is the task of all scientists in their respective fields and subject matters.

There is no doubt about the vast influence of knowledge and beliefs, and their diffusion, upon human behavior. Whatever their shortcomings, the analyses of business statistics for individual businesses and industries, as well as the work on general business cycles, represent an incomparable improvement in systematized knowledge and predictability over what would obtain if no such systematized records were kept. Likewise, it is possible from life tables to predict with great accuracy the frequency and incidence of deaths by age, sex, and other characteristics. If it be objected that death is an event not subject to the "whims" of human "choice" which is supposed to be so fatal in sociological prediction, it may be pointed out that the incidence of marriage, for example, which is alleged to allow such "whims" may also be predicted with great accuracy for populations with adequate records of past experience. The incidence of auto thefts can be predicted with remarkable accuracy from the size of the city.[12] Traffic fluctuations with the time of day, the seasonal fluctuation of relief loads, and probability of student failures in college on the basis of their high school records, are matters of common knowledge and of great practical use to all administrators in the fields concerned. Already the social sciences have a large number of such correlations demonstrably established, and whenever we find relatively intelligent and efficient social administration in any area, it is usually attributable to the existence, and use in that area, of relatively reliable correlations of the type here mentioned.

D. Present Status and Prospects of Sociological Laws

THE SYSTEMATIC DEVELOPMENT of probability tables for social phenomena other than those covered by life tables and other actuarial data is still in its infancy. The pioneer work of Hart [13] and Burgess [14] and the subsequent work of the Gluecks,[15] Vold,[16] Monachesi,[17] and Laune [18] on criminological phenomena, as well as the work of Burgess and Cottrell [19] on family adjustment are, however, most promising attempts to extend the actuarial technic into new and broader fields of human interrelationships. As has frequently been true in the history of the development of scientific laws, the immediate incentive for the attempts here noted is to develop a practical device for the more efficient handling of a specific administrative problem perhaps for a very restricted group. But technics thus developed and applied frequently throw a flood of light upon much more general and fundamental problems.

Early experiments in probability laws were regarded as an amusement and a sport, and were considered as applicable only to gambling devices and games of chance. Today the probability calculus dominates every department of science. The experiments of Clerk Maxwell and Faraday were at the time regarded as curious observations

of doubtful general significance. They turned out to be of fundamental importance to the whole framework of science. At the present
time the attempt to develop, for example, probability tables from
which can be predicted various degrees of adjustment in marriage
is generally regarded as of importance chiefly as a practical device by
which unwise marriages might be avoided, or chiefly as a type of
inquiry designed to throw light on domestic problems. The scientific
by-products of such studies if extensively and intensively carried out
are likely to be much more far-reaching. Reliable probability tables
of degrees of adjustment in marriage would not only yield reliable
data on the relative influence, if any, of all the factors today alleged
to be related to marital adjustment but would yield very valuable
information and hypotheses regarding the more general basis of attraction and repulsion among people, which is probably basic to all
social science.

Perhaps the most frequently urged objection to the possibility of
developing probability tables regarding the more complex social behavior phenomena is the contention that social change would constantly invalidate such tables and that the existence of such tables
and predictions from them would themselves be influences tending to
invalidate predictions from them. If, for example, the indicated probability of failure of a proposed marriage is high, and if this fact together with the reasons for the unfavorable prognosis is made clear
to the contracting parties, might not this knowledge itself operate so
to alter what would otherwise have been the probable result so as to
invalidate the prediction shown by the table? To be quite specific,
suppose the presence of a mother-in-law in the household is shown
to be a hazard in marital adjustment. Might not this demonstrated
fact so alter the customary relationship of all members of a household in which the condition exists, so as largely to vitiate the expectancy as shown by probability tables constructed *before probability tables became a condition affecting marital adjustment?*

That such tables might have considerable effect not only on marriage selection but on the customary weight of other factors in the
marital relationship is undeniable. Neither can it be denied that the
known hazards of such conditions as, for example, overweight may,
as a result of the demonstration of this fact by specific life tables,
and discrimination against such cases by life insurance companies,
induce many people to take active measures to prevent overweight

or to guard against its expected hazards. To the extent that the latter can be done, the life tables based upon experience before such precautions became prevalent, lose their validity. This consequence can be avoided only by continuous revision of the tables basing them upon the most recent data. As a matter of fact, such changes in habit would themselves be only gradual, so that the continual revision of expectancy tables by dropping the data of the earliest years of the period on the basis of which a given table is computed and adding the most recent would probably keep the tables up to date and sensitive to all but the most sudden and revolutionary changes.

This technic is, of course, already worked out to a high degree of flexibility in various forms of insurance. The addition of a night watchman to a factory, for example, calls for a revision in the fire expectancy and a corresponding reduction in the insurance rate. The only sound basis for such reduction is an adequate record of experience with establishments served by night watchmen as contrasted with those not so protected. Actuarial estimates are themselves undoubtedly a major influence in bringing about a change in the probabilities of the events predicted. But this fact has in no way destroyed the soundness of actuarial principles and methods or in their continued practical usefulness.

The extension of these methods into all departments of societal behavior would require the same constant accumulation of experience and the same constant revision of our probability estimates. But at any given time, a statement of the probability of any given event that can be predicted from an actuarial table constitutes a "natural law" of that class of events in the same sense that this expression is now used in physics. All laws of physics likewise hold only upon the stipulated condition that the conditions under which they were formulated (usually laboratory conditions) remain constant.[20] If these conditions change, the law, as a description of what actually occurs under the changed conditions, must be altered.

E. The Instability of Societal Phenomena

THERE WILL DOUBTLESS be those who, while finding the above analysis logically irrefutable, will nevertheless feel that the points of reference from which the laws of physics are derived are nevertheless intrinsically more stable and unchangeable than the corresponding points of reference upon which social scientists must rely. This view derives partly (1) from the assumption previously criticized, namely, that the conventional points of reference in the language of contemporary science are "physical" entities rather than symbolized response categories, and (2) partly from a highly distorted perspective in time and comparability of units in the physical and in the social sciences. The latter is perhaps primarily attributable to a deep-seated anthropocentrism on account of which it is felt that the human life span, or at most the affairs of a local culture, are in the social sciences the counterpart to the solar system, for example, in astronomy.

A favorite method of arguing this point is to refer to the stability of such reference points as the earth's orbit and other astronomical regularities. The argument is that there are no comparably stable frames of reference for social phenomena. Social scientists are fond of pointing to this staggering obstacle as an excuse for the shortcomings of their sciences. Change, it would appear, is a phenomenon encountered only, or at least mainly, in societal phenomena. The point is supported by a wealth of illustrations of the transitory character of human life and institutions, the ups and downs of governments, and other recurring upheavals in technology and culture generally.

It is a fact of common observation that to unaided human senses, at least, the sense of movement or change is always relative to some points of reference. We are not aware of our direction or speed of movement in an airplane unless we see the ground, the clouds, or other not too distant objects. The fluctuations in any phenomena are frequent and violent in proportion to our closeness to the phenomena in time and space. The automobiles immediately before us shoot by at terrific speed; an equally rapidly traveling car two miles away seems to be barely moving at all. As for the movements of the heavenly bodies and the earth itself, we infer them from the different relative positions which they occupy at different times. It follows that the more macroscopic the perspective which we choose, the more apparently stable and invariable will be events within that macrocosm, because it includes within itself the points of reference, without which no sensation of change or instability is possible. If the macrocosm selected is bounded only by the uttermost reaches of human senses, *that* macrocosm would necessarily be stable for there are no points of reference with reference to which its movement or change can be inferred. Indeed, when more powerful telescopes permit the extension of our senses and thus provide new points of reference the erstwhile "stable" macrocosm becomes unstable and astronomers "see" constellations rushing through space at great speed. By use of other instruments and reference points, geologists "see" continents rising and falling. To those of us who spend a brief life-time upon these continents they are stable—sufficiently stable for us to use them as a fixed frame of reference for most of our adjustments. Such also is the stability of the earth's orbit and the earth's movements with reference to it and the heavenly bodies. As John Dewey has said: "As we can discourse of change only in terms of velocity and acceleration which involve relations to other things, so assertion of permanent and enduring is comparative. The stablest thing we can speak of is not free from the conditions set to it by other things." [21]

We postulated in the first chapter that all phenomena of man and culture are entirely contained within the physical cosmos and entirely dependent upon the energy transformations within that cosmos. [22] It follows that man's social universe, not to mention individual cultures, are *part* of that cosmos and are therefore surrounded with points of reference without which, as we have seen above, change cannot be perceived. The smaller the social segment under observation, therefore, the greater will be its instability within the range of discrimination of human senses. As we go beyond that range, for example, into atomic levels, stability reappears (to the unaided senses). In short, both macroscopic and microscopic changes are largely lost to the unaided senses because these senses cannot detect in either case the reference points without which the sensation of motion, change, or stability is impossible.

As a fact and as a difficulty to be reckoned with, this instability is in no way reduced or vitiated by the above analysis, which merely shows the relativity and the nature of our concepts of stability and change. But this analysis does suggest that the instabilities of social phenomena are of the same character as the instabilities of other phenomena which have less than cosmic points of reference. The latter, in fact, include the bulk of the phenomena with which physical science deals. Whatever appears to be the stability of the earth's orbit and the regularity of the motions of heavenly bodies, there is no pretense in physics of any other than statistical regularities and the stability of probabilities. In short, through the development of refined instruments and methods of dealing with *change,* science has achieved some of the same results which theologians and metaphysicians attempted to achieve through postulates of the *unchanging.*

The apparent stability of some of the broader and more "ultimate" (?) points of reference of astronomy, for example, will doubtless continue to inspire envy in a large number of social scientists. It is easy to understand their quest for a corresponding Rock of Ages to which the social sciences can be moored. I have attempted above to point out that the phenomenon in question is actually not inherent in one subject matter as contrasted with another, but that it is the effect of perspective in time and space. From some points of view, this fact in no way affects the significance of the apparent difference. From the point of view here under consideration, namely, the applicability of certain methods of study to societal phenomena, the viewpoint is of fundamental significance.

In conclusion, it may be pointed out that even the major alleged stabilities or constants of astronomy themselves undergo radical transformations in the course of the centuries. It must be remembered that the notion of the earth's orbit is only an improved verbal framework (as compared with the Ptolemaic) within which at present certain observed astronomical behavior-phenomena can be comprehended more adequately. These same phenomena were for many centuries comprehended by a radically different framework. The provincial view that the former was merely a "wrong" notion held by men until the "true" orientation was "discovered" unfortunately still persists quite generally with regard to the nature of scientific formulations. The mounting of a new and powerful telescope which will penetrate millions of light-years hitherto unknown to man is even now under way. (Written in 1938.) May it not reveal vistas and behavior to comprehend which modifications of present astronomical orientations will be necessary? Thus may the stabilities of the foundations of our present universe be transformed and the fundamental instability of all phenomena, or at least of man's response to them, again be demonstrated.

F. Conclusion

THIS AND PRECEDING chapters have attempted to show that the apparent difficulty of applying the methods of natural science to societal phenomena flow not from any intrinsic characteristics of these phenomena but from the retention in the latter field of postulates long since repudiated in the other sciences. Indeed, the postulate of such intrinsic difference as regards man's method of knowing about the two fields of human observation is the principal assumption which must be abandoned if the social studies are ever to become sciences in the sense that physics or chemistry are sciences.

Since Darwin, the abandonment of that postulate has been reluctant but steady. The abandonment of a time-honored postulate and the adoption of a new frame of reference frequently calls for cruel partings with eloquent vocabulary, learned lecture notes, and vested intellectual interests. We try to achieve the transition as gradually as possible in order not to shock the organism too violently by the change. The technic of changing one's postulates usually is to quit talking about postulates entirely until one has developed some verbal facility in the new orientation. Social scientists are in this transition at present. The ways of science attract us strongly both because of the results that can be achieved with science and because of its academic and public prestige. But we also like to retain some beloved articles of our erstwhile faith. The latter frequently embarrasses us, so we try to hide it as much as possible, but continue to use it until we can acquire equipment suitable to the new orientation.[23]

Social scientists are at present engaged in the old attempt to eat their cake and have it too—to be scientific but not to learn any mathematics, to generalize but not to acquire the only technic by which masses of data can be legitimately generalized. They have never explicitly stated the fundamental postulates upon which they proceed and for the most part have refused to face those which indubitably underlie the whole scientific approach. In short, they are engaged in trying to bootleg their nonscientific concepts and frameworks into the law-abiding domain of science.

The postulate that some data are inherently and intrinsically objective or subjective, homogeneous or nonhomogeneous, measurable or nonmeasurable, is in some orientations entirely defensible. The scientific orientation proceeds, however, on a contrary hypothesis, namely, that these categories represent not intrinsic characteristics of data, but different ways of responding to data. All known data have this important characteristic in common: They become known through human reactions. I hold that by certain methods, through certain inventable operations, the subjective becomes objective, the nonhomogeneous becomes homogeneous, the "complex" becomes "simple," and the nonmeasurable becomes measurable.

From this point of view, I find Margenau's statement in another connection the inevitable conclusion. He says:

"If the fundamental thesis of quantum mechanics is correct, *all* physical observations form a probability aggregate, that is, a set of data to which the probability calculus can be applied. . . . And if, as is frequently supposed, the data of all exact empirical sciences are basically physical, we are confronted with the possibility that the entire physical world [in which I include the social—G. L.], ultimately resolves itself into a set of events joined merely by the rules of the probability calculus." [24]

If this is the nature of contemporary science, then I think the methods by which scientific laws are to be achieved in the social sciences were correctly summarized more than fifty years ago by Henry L. Moore in his *Laws of Wages* (pp. 4–5), when he said:

"The problems of natural science have required the invention of a calculus of mass phenomena that will probably yield its best results when applied to the material of the social sciences. The wealth of the statistical material . . . is itself a source of embarrassment. To utilize it for scientific purposes, it must be described in brief, summary formulae, and these formulae must be arranged upon a plan of increasing complexity so that it will be possible to pass from accurate descriptions of mass aggregates to the relations between the aggregates themselves."

The ends of science are the same in all fields, namely, to arrive at verifiable generalizations as to the sequences of events. Any methods that yield these results are permitted in all the sciences. It happens, however, that generalization implies applicability to *numbers of cases,* and hence all scientific laws, including those arrived at by so-called qualitative analysis, ultimately rely for their scientific validity

upon the fact that they can be, and have been, corroborated in numbers of cases. The trend toward the adoption of mathematical technics as any science matures is, therefore, not due to any compulsion
to imitate any other science. The compulsion flows from the nature
of accurate generalization, which is the essence of science.

In short, we adopt no concepts or mathematical technics *because*
they are used in other sciences. We adopt them, if at all, because
they are effective tools in reaching admittedly desired ends. The latter
criterion also allows full scope for the invention by social scientists
of new symbolic systems or procedures uniquely adapted to their
special problems. The postulate of the ultimate unity of all science
is doubtless implicit in the principle of parsimony. But this principle
may just as readily call for modifications in the physical sciences as
in the social, if the principles of the former are found too narrow to
encompass the latter.

Finally, we recognize that the approach we advocate in this volume
assumes technological developments within the sociological sciences
which will make possible and perhaps easy many tasks which
from the standpoint of our present technics may seem impossible or
of staggering difficulty.[25] Sociologists have always been conspicuous
in calling attention to the revolutionary effects of technological developments in practically all departments of life including the other
sciences. Where sociology itself is concerned, the assumption seems
rather to have been that the concepts, technics, and types of scholar-
ship of the great social philosophers represent the only valid method
of attack. Sociology is perhaps the only science in which a leader of a
century ago would not be greatly handicapped if he should suddenly
come to life again. The technological developments during the same
period within all other sciences have completely transformed them.
The most distinguished scholar of a century ago could not read even
an elementary treatise on these sciences. Can it be that sociology
is the one unique department of life and of thought where further
technological development is not possible?

G. Notes

1. The same reasoning would hold for Newton's modification of this
(Kepler's) "law" to the effect that if no force acts on a body in motion,
it continues to move uniformly in a straight line.

2. A. Comte, *Positive Philosophy*, (Translated by H. Martineau) Trübner, 1853, II, p. 537.

3. "An axiom . . . means a self-evident truth that is . . . one that will be immediately accepted by every intelligent person. A postulate . . . is an assumption or hypothesis, i.e., something agreed upon for the sake of argument. (P. 484.) One often hears the statement that in any deductive system, all the theorems are implicitly contained in the postulates; or, in other words, that the process of deduction from the postulates never yields anything essentially new. (P. 493.) The impression though widely prevalent is quite erroneous. In every live deductive theory, novelties are constantly appearing, due to the introduction of new definitions by ingenious and original investigators. These new combinations are not implicitly contained in the postulates, but reflect the intelligent interest of some creative human agent. The postulates are like traffic laws: they prohibit traveling in wrong directions, but they do not provide any motive power. Similar remarks apply to the choice of the postulates themselves. The postulates adopted as the basis of any system constitute the definition of that system, within its universe of discourse. . . . The technique of the postulatioral method effects a great saving in mental effort, in connection with definitions, just as it does in connection with theorems. . . . In other so-called exact sciences, like physics and chemistry, only a very few basic concepts are required, all the other concepts in the science being defined in terms of the fundamental ones (as velocity in terms of length and time, work in terms of force and distance, etc.). It is due largely to this fact that these sciences have acquired as much exactness as they have." (P. 494.) (E. V. Huntington, "The Method of Postulates," *Phil. of Sci.,* IV, Oct., 1937, pp. 482-495.) On the general subject of scientific laws of societal phenomena see A. Lesser, "Research Procedure and Laws of Culture," *Phil. of Sci.,* VI, July, 1939, pp. 345-355.

See also the notable work of Clark Hull in applying this method in the field of psychology. ("The Conflicting Psychologies of Learning—A Way Out." *Psychol. Rev.,* XLII, Nov., 1935, pp. 491-516.) There will be those who feel that the "elaborate" demonstration of "what everyone knows" is nothing more than an attempt to "imitate" some other science, or at best mere pedantry. The appeal to "what everyone knows" has always been a trump card in the hand of the obscurantist. Nothing seemed more self-evident than the parallel axiom before Einstein's epoch-making abandonment of it. The scientist does not consider his task completed, but only begun, when he has achieved a personal conviction that a certain relationship holds. The objective recording of *the steps, the operations,* linguistic (logical), or other manipulatory procedures, *through which the conclusion was reached,* so that others may corroborate them, remains his major task. The obligation of the scientist to make clear the steps by which he concludes that the earth is round is in no way abrogated by the fact that all people may already agree to the conclusion. Scientific contributions frequently consist chiefly of laying bare—rendering explicit—the steps and operations by which a relationship, long observed, can be rationally (logically) explained. Only when these sequences are thus rendered explicit can the *principle* which a phenomenon illustrates be derived, generalized, and applied to other situations, for purposes of prediction and for general economy of effort in interpreting the plethora of individual events with which our senses are bombarded. Only when the principle governing a phenomenon is thus deduced from known data, can we with safety assume that our adjustments based on such data will also be adequate in similar situations as yet unexperienced.

4. R. M. MacIver, *Community,* Macmillan, 1931, p. 417. MacIver's further development of this subject is entirely compatible with the position here taken and is indeed a necessary analysis prior to the type of definition and measurement here advocated.

5. *Ibid.,* p. 231.

6. Eleanor Bisbee, "Objectivity in the Social Sciences," *Phil. of Sci.,* IV, July, 1937, pp. 371-382.

7. *Ibid.,* p. 378.

8. K. E. Boulding, "Is Economics Necessary?" *Scientific Monthly,* April, 1949.

9. *Ibid.,* p. 235.

10. I have elsewhere pointed out that "free will" and "the will of God" are subject to scientific study and prediction in the same way. See *Can Science Save Us,* 2nd ed., p. 107.

11. S. I. Hayakawa, "On Communication with the Soviet Union, Etc.," *A Review of General Semantics,* Vol. 17, No. 4, 1960. Pp. 389-400. See also "Civil Defense, Democracy, and the Self-Destroying Prophecy," *The American Behavioral Scientist,* October, 1962, pp. 3-6.

12. J. Hall, *Theft, Law, and Society,* Little, Brown, 1935, p. 242.

13. H. Hart, "Predicting Parole Success," *Journal of Criminal Law and Criminology,* XIV, Nov., 1923, pp. 405-413.

14. E. W. Burgess, "Factors Determining Success or Failure on Parole," in *Study of the Indeterminate Sentence and Parole in Illinois,* by A. A. Bruce *et al.,* Supt. of Pub. Documents, Springfield, 1928.

15. S. and E. T. Glueck, *Five Hundred Criminal Careers,* Knopf, 1930.

16. George B. Vold, *Prediction Methods and Parole,* The Sociological Press, Hanover, New Hampshire, 1931.

17. E. D. Monachesi, *Prediction Factors in Probation,* The Sociological Press, Hanover, New Hampshire, 1932.

18. F. F. Laune, *Predicting Criminality,* Northwestern University Studies in the Social Sciences, No. 1, Northwestern University, 1936.

19. E. W. Burgess and L. S. Cottrell, Jr., "The Prediction of Adjustment in Marriage," *American Sociological Review,* I, Oct., 1936, pp. 737-751.

20. For an example of a scientific law in sociology as verified by controlled experiment, see S. C. Dodd and Marilyn McCurtain, "The Logistic Law of Communication," *Symposia Studies No. 8 of the National Institute of Social and Behavioral Science, Series Research in Social Psychology,* Washington, D.C., September, 1961.

21. John Dewey, *Experience and Nature,* Norton, 1925, p. 70. See also pp. 71-72.

22. For further development of this point, see Chapters I and VI of the First Edition.

23. V. Pareto has analyzed this process in terms of residues, derivations, and nonlogical thoughtways. See his *The Mind and Society,* Harcourt, 1935, I.

24. *Journal of the American Statistical Association,* XXXI, March, 1936, p. 27. Discussion by Henry Margenau of paper by E. Nagel, "The Meaning of Probability."

25. The invention of computing machinery and new mathematical approaches since this was written in 1938, is of revolutionary significance.

Chapter V

EPILOGUE

TWENTY-FIVE YEARS have elapsed since the foregoing chapters were written. During that time sociology as well as most of the other social sciences have undergone rapid development in methods of research as well as in attempts at more comprehensive theorizing. The latter development has consisted of constructing systems of concepts intended to be more or less unique and comprehensive from the point of view of their respective authors and followers. At the same time there has been a growing interest in common elements and convergences to be found in the various proposed systems.[1]

In what direction, if any, has sociological theory developed in recent decades? Are the developments wholly divergent and incompatible, or are there notable convergences in the apparent variability? Are the convergences, if any, notably in the direction of natural science, or in some other direction? This Epilogue attempts to explore two contemporary conceptual schemes from this point of view.[2]

We shall attempt below to show that certain theoretical formulations and research approaches that have until recently been regarded as mutually hostile, if not wholly incompatible, are, according to recent statements of them, highly compatible and strongly convergent. Further, this convergence has been achieved mainly through an evolution of two principal schools of thought in the direction of the theory and methods of natural science.[3] This thesis is documented by references chiefly to the conceptual schemes and methods of Talcott Parsons and those of S. C. Dodd.

I have already called attention in another paper [4] to the coalescence during the past decade in personnel and in ideology in two leading graduate schools, namely, Columbia and Harvard. I also called attention to the shift in certain quarters from skepticism regarding quantitative methods and especially sociological scales and related matters to an enthusiastic appreciation of the brilliant work of Lazarsfeld, Guttman, and Stouffer in this field. In the present essay I will further illustrate this trend by an examination of the most recent statements of Parsons and his associates as found in *Working Papers in the Theory of Action.*[5]

The most general complaint against Parsons' theoretical formulations has been, as one writer has recently said, that it "frequently has been regarded as too difficult or overtly abstract for utilization in research." [6] In view of this widely felt difficulty, the following statement must be regarded as extremely important:

"The essential relations which we wish to discuss are, with the exception of the involvement of symbolism, schematically represented in Figure 3 [of *Working Papers.*] This shows that *it is possible to regard the categories of interaction process developed by Bales and the motivational paradigm developed by Parsons, as, in all essentials, different ways of conceptualizing the same thing.* The mode of organization of the scheme revolves about the 'functional problems of social systems' put forward by Bales, and the pattern variables of Parsons and Shils, put together in a specific combination; the two in this context turning out to mean essentially the same thing." [7] (Italics mine.)

My reason for regarding the above statement of such major significance is that the identification of Parsons' terminology with Bales's categories gives us, I believe for the first time, operational specifications of the meaning of these terms. Bales's categories were developed in concrete, objective research and are subject to the usual empirical checks of reliability and validity. Accordingly, we have here for the first time the basic categories of a widely studied system defined operationally so that they can be used by different investigators with some assurance of their designating the same referents. That is, Bales and other properly trained observers can agree with considerable reliability that a given instance of interactional behavior is to be designated by one rather than another of his categories. Accordingly, they are wholly compatible with the neopositivists' requirements so far as definitions of categories are concerned. The possible larger usefulness of these particular categories in the development of sociological theory is another matter. That is a subject for future determination on the basis of results secured in actual research.

Before proceeding with a more detailed analysis of the parallels between the Parsons-Bales categories and those of Dodd, let us observe first how certain subsidiary problems that have been the subject of much controversy fall out or recede to the background as the more rigorous meaning of the categories is specified. Speaking of his twelve categories, Bales says:

"The set of categories is held to form a logically exhaustive classification system. Every act that occurs is classified into one of the twelve categories. All of the categories are positively defined—that is, none of them is treated as a residual or wastebasket category for 'leftovers.' With competent observers and hard training, correlations between observers ranging from .75 to .95 can be obtained." [8]

Obviously, the old argument over operational definitions is here immediately relegated to the background. Description and repeated observation of the interaction process by Bales's laboratory observers has required the factoring of the interaction and the rigorous specification of what segment of behavior is to be designated by a particular category. The specifications and delimitations prescribed for observers in the laboratory instructions *constitute* operational definitions of the categories.

And what about quantification? In the first place, if certain behavior occurs in varying degrees, quantitative symbols are convenient to designate degree. Also, after having observed and described a large number of group-interaction situations, the question of the frequency of recurrence and nonrecurrence arises. Some well-established statistical methods are routinely invoked by Bales to answer these questions. New techniques to suit new types of observation will doubtless be developed from time to time. In short, the traditional argument about operational definitions and quantification, which at least one writer designates as major ingredients of a school of theory called neopositivism,[9] is quietly taken care of as incidental in actual scientific work. They have nothing to do with substantive theory in any field of science but are generally accepted methods of scientific procedure. Accordingly, it is absurd to set them down as the special property or characteristic of neopositivism or any other sociological theory.

Operational definitions and quantitative techniques are not inherent in some schools of scientific thought and lacking in others. They are semantic techniques of more perfect or more precise communication, not subjects to be adopted or rejected at the outset according to what theory one decides to pursue. Thus, one by one, the major subjects of debate during the last two decades in sociological theory are quietly laid to rest or reduced to their proper incidental significance. That is, when *predictability* is accepted as the criterion of scientific work, certain other questions become purely a matter of deciding what means and methods contribute most efficiently and reliably to the stipulated end. Operational definitions and quantitative techniques are, by this criterion, demonstrably most efficient. This does not mean either in sociology or in physics that all other concepts, including "primitive" and "literary" ones, are prohibited. They will continue to be used and will be defined with whatever degree of operationality is demanded by the results sought.

The same may be said of much of the other argument about the merits of different alleged "schools" of sociological theory. We hear about behaviorism, positivism, neopositivism, "functionalism," and, as a gratuitous insult to all the others, an "analytical" school.[10] Parsons, for example, devotes a hundred pages in his *Structure of Social Action* to a discussion of positivism and assures us that "it will be maintained and the attempt made in considerable detail to prove that in this sense [*as a general framework for understanding human behavior*] *all of the variations of positivistic social thought constitute untenable positions for both empirical and methodological reasons.*" [11] To be sure, it never becomes very clear what the monstrous doctrine is or who represents the various categories and subcategories of it. But traditional notions of now largely mythical sociological "schools" still persist. Thus, Timasheff, writing in 1955, still finds at least three recognizable "elements" that characterize the neopositivist theoretical framework: "quantitativism," "behaviorism," and "pragmatic philosophy." [12] By a sort of common consent, other characteristics which are usually also designated as characterizing this "school" are neglect of the "psychic component" and a preoccupation with or "aping" the natural sciences.

Consider now in the light of the above characterization the recent exposition of their theory by Parsons and his associates. Even a cursory examination of Chapter III of *Working Papers* is illuminating from the point of view of what I have somewhat conservatively called "convergence" in sociological theory in the direction of positivism. The title alone of the Parsons-Bales chapter should be alarming to those who apparently believe that, if certain words used in chemistry or physics are also employed in sociology, it constitutes strong presumptive evidence that the author is a "natural science" sociologist who proposes "to force sociology into the framework of physics." Well, the title of the Parsons-Bales chapter in question reads "The Dimensions of Action-Space." Dodd's title, "Dimensions of Society" (1942), created agitation because it was felt in some circles that the word "dimensions," since it figures prominently in physics, cannot properly be used in sociology. Today it is permissible to speak of social dimensions, especially when we *measure* certain aspects or characteristics of social behavior. Sociologists today are interested in what one can do with a terminology or a framework, regardless of where it has come from. But, if the above be regarded as possibly merely an accident of terminology, consider the following statements toward the end of the chapter:

"If all this, which frankly involves a speculative element at present, is correct, then it would seem likely that there is a very important analogy between the scheme we have developed in this paper and the classical mechanics. If this supposition stands up to critical testing of a variety of sorts, it is evident that it should turn out to have far-reaching implications in that it should open up possibilities of quantitative as well as qualitative systematization which are far beyond those which the sciences of action have yet attained.

For convenience we present succinct statements of the four generalized conditions of equilibrium or laws just reviewed as follows:

1. *The Principle of Inertia:* A given process of action will continue unchanged in rate and direction unless impeded or deflected by opposing motivational forces.

2. *The Principle of Action and Reaction:* If, in a system of action, there is a change in the *direction* of a process, it will tend to be balanced by a *complementary change which is equal in motivational force and opposite in direction.*

3. *The Principle of Effort:* Any change in the rate of an action process is directly proportional to the *magnitude* of the motivational force applied or withdrawn.

4. *The Principle of System-Integration:* Any *pattern* element (*mode of organization* of components) within a *system* of action will tend to be confirmed in its place within the system or to be eliminated from the system (extinguished) as a function of its contribution to the integrative balance of the system." [13]

It will be seen that the first three of these proposed laws are identical with those of classical mechanics, and the fourth is definitely of the *same type*. I am not here concerned with validity or scientific value; I am merely interested in calling attention to the fact that, regardless of their merit, this is the type of formulation which fifteen years ago would have been greeted with howls of protest as representing attempts "to force sociology into the framework of physics." Yet it would be difficult to find more striking examples than these of a convergence of sociological theory and terminology in the direction of what has hitherto been called neopositivism, behaviorism, and "natural science."

Now the proponents of sociology as a natural science have never held that the terminology and methods or theories of other sciences were to be adopted in sociology *because* they had been found useful in other sciences. On the other hand, we have said, and we do say, that in our search for hypotheses and for suggestions regarding methods we will and should look first to the analogous problems which we have already successfully solved. A fairly substantial victory has been won for this point of view during the last fifteen years, and social scientists stand greatly to profit from it. Incidentally, in the above formulation Parsons and his associates have in effect returned to the cradle of positivism. Auguste Comte in his *Positive Philosophy* (1859) asserted that Newton's three laws of motion applied to social phenomena. It is true that his discussion of the point was more philosophical than mathematical. But Stuart C. Dodd as early as 1934 proposed definite operational methods of remedying the shortcoming by submitting the following formulation:

"To paraphrase Newton's laws of motion in sociological terms gives:

1. Every group continues in its present status or social process until compelled by a force to change that status or process.

"A version preferred by the writer as implying less of a metaphysical assumption and more of a simple agreement to standardize a definition is:

1. (*a*) Whatever changes the status of a group or its process in rate or direction is called a social force.
2. Change of rate of a social process is proportional to the social force and takes place along the line of the scale in which the force is measured.
3. Forces and their total resistances are equal and opposite.

"These principles in social terms are not seen as postulates of the ultimate metaphysical nature of society and its functioning. They are modestly viewed as simple proposals to standardize the meaning of social force and the units for measuring it. . . . Force thus is not a thing nor an active agent as it is in the popular view. Scientifically it is *that which* produces a measured effect. It is a pure invented concept justified by its usefulness in dealing with phenomena. If this is understood, forces may be spoken of as political forces, or economic forces, or psychological forces, etc., as convenient designations of the agencies producing forces, *i.e.*, stimulating people to respond." [14]

It is unnecessary to elaborate upon the striking similarity between Dodd's formulation and that by Parsons and his associates as given above. It is of great interest to note, however, that much of the tremendously elaborate and voluminous work of Parsons can in the end be distilled into this historic formulation. This is not to minimize the importance of the steps, however circuitous they may seem, by which Parsons arrived at this conclusion. It is the possibility of the translation, as admitted by Parsons, that is important.

I have been concerned above with certain large and general trends and convergences in the theoretical positions of Parsons and Dodd. Fortunately, in this case we need not become involved in any controversy as to who was influenced by whom, because each author readily grants his inability to read the other's works, at least until recently.

Since Bales has provided the key to a more objective understanding of Parsons' categories, a more detailed comparison now may be made between them and the categories of Dodd.

Chart I shows the principal parallels between the *general* systems of Parsons and Dodd. The texts referred to corroborate the validity of the parallelism exhibited in Chart I—a parallelism which seems genuine and striking.

CHART I

A COMPARISON OF THE GENERAL CATEGORIES OF PARSONS AND DODD

Parsons' *Action* [15]	Dodd's *Transact* [16]
1. *Actors* a) Individuals or collectivities b) Subject-object	1. *People* (Who?) a) Persons or groups b) Actors-reactors
2. *Situation* a) Social objects (persons and groups) b) Non-social objects (physical and cultural)	2. *Time, space,* and *residual factors* (When?) (Where?) (How?) a) Symbolic factors (including symbols of persons and groups) b) Material factors (physical and cultural)
3. *Orientation of (1) to (2)* a) Motivational orientation: cognitions, cathexis, evaluative modes b) Value orientations: cognitive, appreciative, moral	3. *Actions* and *values* [17] (orientation relating [1] to [2]) (Doing what? Why?) a) Motivational orientation—actions (in knowing, feeling, doing modes) b) Value orientation—standards or desiderata in knowing, feeling, doing modes

When we turn to a more detailed comparison of the Bales-Parsons-Dodd categories as applied to the highly restricted and simple laboratory situation for which Bales's categories were adopted, the parallels may be less clear because each author uses brief, general terms from folk language to designate aspects or dimensions of quite complex social situations. The parallelism between the Bales-Parsons categories, as attested by them, is exhibited in Figure 3 of their *Working Papers*.[18] In our Chart II we compare the categories of Bales and Dodd. As Chart II shows, Dodd's categories are generated by cross-classifying two generalized dimensions, viz.: (1) action in three modes (doing, feeling, knowing) against (2) interaction in four degrees (positive in two degrees and negative in two degrees). The parallels in the meaning of the categories will be more striking in some cases than in others, but it must be remembered that the full equivalence (or lack thereof) can be exhibited only after a full exposition of each system and the specific meaning adopted by each author for the terms employed in the chart. Also it must be noted that the *generality* of Dodd's categories, as compared with those of Bales, which are adapted to a specific laboratory situation, necessarily results in considerable disparity of terminology especially when terms are taken apart from their context as in Chart II. The same is true also of the Parsons-Bales categories. The degree of actual correspondence in the three systems deserves more intensive inquiry.

Since the experimental situation for which Bales developed his categories is highly circumscribed and controlled, their adequacy for more complex and general situations is as yet undetermined. The more comprehensive systems of Parsons and Dodd profess, of course, to provide a framework for the analysis of any human social situation whatever. Most of Parsons' work deals with these more general situations, and Dodd has experimented with the applicability of his categories to very much broader social contexts as described in his published research.[19] More to the point in the present comparison is Dodd's application of his categories to original behavior situations.[20]

Incidentally, both systems achieve a high degree of parsimony in that Parsons and Bales have only twelve categories which are held to be logically exhaustive, whereas Dodd proposes eight concepts, one of which, however, is residual. The system claims to provide a parsimonious way of describing in terms of eight basic concepts, and in other derivative concepts defined in terms of the original eight, the sociological essence of any situation represented by such a question as "Who does what, why, when, where, and how?" Bales's categories have so far been applied only to the communicative aspects of a group discussion under laboratory conditions. Their validity in larger and more varied situations remains to be demonstrated.

It is not the primary purpose of the present paper to attempt prematurely to evaluate one set of categories as against another: that will come about incidentally as research and experiment continue. We are interested here primarily in calling attention to a considerable fundamental parallelism in two systems hitherto assumed by many to represent incompatible systems.

CHART II

CONVERGENCE OF INTERACTION CATEGORIES BETWEEN BALES AND DODD
(AND PARSONS)

			MODES OF SPEECH BEHAVIOR					
			"I DO ..."		"I FEEL ..."		"I KNOW ..."	
			DODD	BALES	DODD	BALES	DODD	BALES
INTEGRATIVE INTERACTION	POSITIVE	STRONG	Strongly integrative doing	1	Strongly integrative feeling	2	Strongly integrative knowing	3
				Shows solidarity		Shows tension release		Agrees
		WEAK	Weakly integrative doing	4	Weakly integrative feeling	5	Weakly integrative knowing	6
				Gives suggestion		Gives opinion		Gives orientation
	NEGATIVE	STRONG	Weakly disintegrative doing	9	Weakly disintegrative feeling	8	Weakly disintegrative knowing	7
				Asks for suggestion		Asks for opinion		Asks for orientation
		WEAK	Strongly disintegrative doing	12	Strongly disintegrative feeling	11	Strongly disintegrative knowing	10
				Shows antagonism		Shows tension		Disagrees

A. Notes

1. See, for example, Charles and Zona Loomis, *Modern Social Theories,* Van Nostrand, 1961.

2. Adapted from G. A. Lundberg, "Some Convergences in Sociological Theory," *American Journal of Sociology,* Vol. 62, July, 1956, pp. 21-27.

3. The term "natural science" is here used instead of "positivism" and "neopositivism" because of the ambiguity of the latter terms. (See Chapter 3, Section B.) On the other hand, the "theory and methods of natural science" can be relatively sharply defined, and are here defined, as the general position expounded in the *International Encyclopedia of Unified Science.* For further discussion of this subject, see G. A. Lundberg, "The Natural Science Trend in Sociology," *American Journal of Sociology,* Vol. 61, November, 1955, pp. 191-202.

4. *Ibid.* In this paper I have dealt at some length also with the work of P. H. Furfey, *The Scope and Method of Sociology,* Harper, 1953.

5. T. Parsons, R. F. Bales, and E. A. Shils, *Working Papers in the Theory of Action,* Free Press, 1953, Ch. III.

6. N. S. Timasheff, *Sociological Theory: Its Nature and Growth,* Doubleday & Co., 1955, p. 239.

7. Parsons, Bales, and Shils, *op. cit.,* p. 71.

8. Paul F. Lazarsfeld and Morris Rosenberg (editors), *The Language of Social Research,* Free Press, 1955, p. 349.

9. N. F. Timasheff, "Sociological Theory Today," *American Catholic Sociological Review,* XI, March, 1950, p. 26.

10. Timasheff, *Sociological Theory: Its Nature and Growth, op. cit.,* Ch. VIII. Timasheff classifies Parsons as among the "analytic" sociologists, the other representatives of which are Sorokin, MacIver, and Znaniecki. T. F. O'Dea ("The Sociology of Religion," *American Catholic Sociological Review,* June, 1954), however, attacks Parsons as a positivist.

11. T. Parsons, *The Structure of Social Action,* Second Edition, Free Press, 1949, p. 42. (Italics in the original.) Parsons outlines (p. 79) two principal types of positivism, "radical" and "statistical," the latter with two subclasses, "individualistic" and "sociologistic," with four subcategories of the latter. How many varieties and subvarieties of "positivism" there may be and who may be their proponents I do not know. On the other hand, the philosophical foundations of natural science as expounded in the various monographs of the *International Encyclopedia of Unified Science* provide a relatively well-defined universe of discourse.

12. Timasheff, *op. cit.,* pp. 137-138.

13. Parsons, Bales, and Shils, *op. cit.,* pp. 102-103.

14. S. C. Dodd, *A Controlled Experiment on Rural Hygiene in Syria,* American Press, 1934, pp. 216-217. See also his *Dimensions of Society,* Macmillan Co., 1942, p. 744, where essentially the same formulation is repeated.

15. See T. Parsons, E. A. Shils, *et al., Toward a General Theory of Action,* Harvard University Press, 1951, pp. 56-60. Also T. Parsons, R. F. Bales, and E. Shils, *Working Papers in the Theory of Action,* Free Press, 1953, Ch. III, especially pp. 162-172.

16. See S. C. Dodd, *Systematic Social Science,* Social Science Series, No. 16, American University of Beirut, 1947. Also S. C. Dodd, "A Predictive Theory of Opinion," *Public Opinion Quarterly,* XX, Fall, 1956. Full report: S. C. Dodd and Marilyn McCurtain, "The Logistic Law in Communication," *Symposia Studies No. 8 of the National Institute of Social and Behavioral Science, Series Research in Social Psychology,* Washington, D.C., September, 1961. (Example of scientific law in social science as verified by controlled experiment.)

17. The six categories italicized represent Dodd's basic factors of a *transact,* or the chief *classes of dimensions* of any social situation. We have attempted to fit Dodd's categories into Parsons' rather than vice versa, in which case the presentation of Dodd's system would be somewhat different, as indicated in the works cited.

18. *Working Papers, op. cit.,* p. 74.

19. See the material analyzed in Dodd, *Dimensions of Society.*

20. For examples see the following: "Dimensions of a Poll," *International Journal of Opinion and Attitudes Research,* Vol. III, No. 3 (Fall, 1949); "On All-or-None Elements and Mathematical Models for Sociologists," *American Sociological Review,* Vol. XVII, No. 2 (April, 1952); "Can the Social Scientist Serve Two Masters?" *Research Studies of the State College of Washington,* Vol. XXI, No. 3 (September, 1953); and "A Predictive Theory of Opinion," *op. cit.*

AUTHOR INDEX

SUBJECT INDEX

Ability, 93

Abstract and concrete phenomena, 39, 40

Abstracting, 98

Adjustment: defined, 1; science as a technic of, 1-4

Aptitude, 93

Aristotelian logic, 54

Attitude, 65, 93

Axioms, 138, 158; and postulates, 158

Capitalism, 54

Case studies vs. statistical methods, 55

Categories: as generalized habits, 19-22; as responses of man, 21

Choice, 7

Classification of sciences, 101-8; and hierarchies, 101-3

Communism, 54

Computational machinery, 93

Concept, and percept, 43

Concrete and abstract phenomena, 39-40

Corollaries of science, 5 ff.

Correlation, 58

Criteria of scientific theories, 108

Culture, meaning of, 129

Cybernetics, 93

Deduction-induction dichotomy, 55

Definition: and measurement, 64-67; of situation, 101

Democracy, 54

Dichotomies, mischievous role of, 55

Dictators, 54

"Economic man," 144-45

Emotion, 7

Ends, 7, 39

Equilibrium, 1, 100-101

Ethics and science, 24-35

Euclidian geometry, 56

"Existence," relativity of, 10-13

Experience, 7

Experimentation, 145-47

Fascism, 54

Fear, 8

Feeling, 7

Field concept, 112-21

Frames of reference, 100; as habit systems, 100; sources of, 108-9; variety of, 100

Function-structure dichotomy, 55

Game theory, 93

Geisteswissenschaften, 8

Generalization, scientific, 61-64

Geometry, Euclidian, 56

Gestalt psychology, 63

Habit systems, 100-101

Hate, 8

Heredity-environment dichotomy, 55